PENNINE WAYS
Edale to Kirk Yetholm for the Independent Walker

John Gillham

Maps by
Jeremy Ashcroft

The Crowood Press

First published in 1994 by
The Crowood Press Ltd
Ramsbury, Marlborough
Wiltshire SN8 2HR

British Library Cataloguing in Publication Data

A catalogue record of this book is available from the British Library.

ISBN 1 85223 841 0

Picture Credits.

Unless otherwise credited the photographs are by the author.

Acknowledgements

I would like to thank those who have helped me in the production of this book. Phil Iddon has taken some lovely photographs in the Yorkshire Dales and Northern Pennines. Jeremy Ashcroft provided the excellent maps. Graham Thompson helped me with his superb photo of the Kinder Downfall. Bill Burlton of the Forestry Enterprize at Bellingham gave me a great deal of very useful information about the plantations of Kielder. I must also thank everyone at Peak Processing (Sheffield), who processed my transparencies with consistently good quality and in double-quick time. Last but not least, special thanks must go to my wife, Nicola, who has taken three of the photographs used in the book and accompanied me on countless trips in all sorts of weather.

Front Cover: The Upper Derwent Valley.
Frontispiece: By the canal at East Marton.
Page 6: The Gorple Stones on the hills above Burnley.

Printed and bound by Paramount Printing Group, Hong Kong.

CONTENTS

INTRODUCTION

In 1935 Tom Stephenson told the world of his dream - the creation of a long-distance footpath over the length of the Pennines. The revolutionary idea caught the public's imagination. Twenty-nine years later, after a mass trespass, Acts of Parliament and much hard work, the dream was realized. The Pennine Way, as it was named, spanned two hundred and fifty miles (400km) between Edale in Derbyshire and Kirk Yetholm, a little-known hamlet over the Scottish border. Many thousands have since followed in Tom Stephenson's footsteps, more often than not with their heads buried in A. Wainwright's little green book (Tom's book was never as popular).

Were it not for the cajoling of my nephew, whose lifetime ambition it was, I would never have dreamed of following the hordes on the Pennine Way. After completing my book, *Snowdonia To The Gower* I was looking for a new challenge and I was finally persuaded to undertake the route. Although there were sections in definite need of improvement I thoroughly enjoyed the experience, especially in the regions of the Yorkshire Dales.

On walking the 'Way' it became obvious that it had become the victim of its own success and the more popular and sensitive sections have become eyesores and quagmires. The severity of the erosion has been worrying the various authorities for a long time. To protect the fragile landscapes in a sympathetic manner is a difficult if not impossible task. In the past some of the efforts have been more of a blight on the landscape than the erosion itself and certainly not in keeping with the wilderness theme of the walk. Many of the worst of the trouble areas are sited close to the trans-Pennine roads. Here the routes, highlighted by Pennine Way signs, are indelibly etched on to the landscape by the likes of duckboards or horrible gravel highways. Even great-grandma can walk them and does - to the new quagmires that have formed at the end of the duckboards!

Perhaps the best option to save the Pennine Way is to declassify the route and promote the concept that to scale the Pennines from Edale to Kirk Yetholm is to walk the Pennine Way, whichever route is chosen. *Pennine Ways* is my offering to this concept - an offering to the independent spirit looking for new and less damaged ways to tackle these beautiful hills. If there is a proliferation of routes over the hills then surely the pressure on each one is lessened.

I decided to base the book on the official 'Way', adding my routes as alternatives. It would be churlish of me to describe one long alternative in isolation and then try claim that it was the superior one. I have tried, wherever possible, to interweave the various routes to meet at convenient accommodation centres in the valleys. This allows infinite options for combining the various official and alternative routes in an individual interpretation.

The first three chapters of the book cover the gritstone terrain which epitomizes the energy-sapping nature of the walk. Outside the dry summer months it can be a harsh introduction, and many fail as their spirits plummet in the quagmires that typify the high moors of the Dark Peak and South Pennines. The more resilient and intrepid travellers will plod on, undeterred, through a wonderland of weird-shaped gritstone boulders and outcrops. When the peat dries, becoming springy and flaky, some may wonder what the fuss is about. Even the infamous Black Hill becomes a doddle.

If the weather is bad my lower level alternative via the Derwent Valley Reservoirs and Howden Moors is superior. It spends less time on the tops and yet still bites deep into the inner recesses of the high moors to the east of Bleaklow. By missing out Black Hill the route traces the gritstone cliff-tops of Saddleworth and Blackstone Edge. Firm paths reveal wide views over the mill towns of Greater Manchester.

I have to say that the stretch between Calderdale's Stoodley Pike and the Haworth Moors is a favourite of mine. One is never far from civilization and the hills have been partially tamed over the years by the efforts of hill farmers, mill owners and reservoir builders but there is a sense of stark romance emanating from the remnants of past industries - you can inhale the atmos-

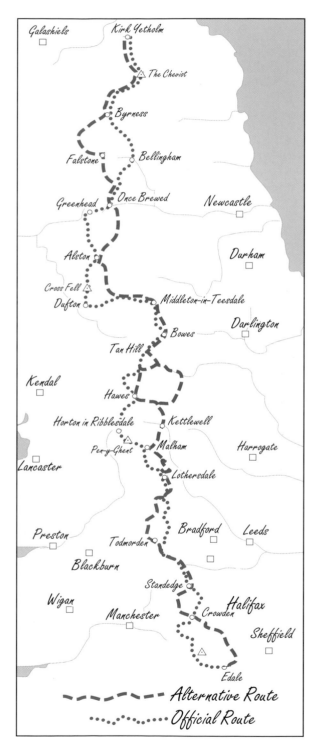

Galashiels
Kirk Yetholm
The Cheviot
Byrness
Falstone
Bellingham
Greenhead
Once Brewed
Newcastle
Alston
Durham
Cross Fell
Dufton
Middleton-in-Teesdale
Darlington
Bowes
Tan Hill
Kendal
Hawes
Horton in Ribblesdale
Kettlewell
Pen-y-Ghent
Malham
Harrogate
Lancaster
Lothersdale
Preston
Bradford
Leeds
Todmorden
Blackburn
Standedge
Wigan
Halifax
Manchester
Crowden
Sheffield
Edale

– – – Alternative Route
•••••• Official Route

phere of *Wuthering Heights* and *Jane Eyre* on every hill-top. There is one nagging doubt along this route how-ever - are those hills on the western skyline a little high-er perhaps? Indeed they are - and tougher to boot. My alternative route here shirks nought and plots a bolder course over these summits from the wild expanses of Rough Hill and Inchfield Moor through to Black Hameldon and Boulsworth Hill. The views of Pendle Hill, the east Lancashire industrial conurbation and the peaks of the Yorkshire Dales are superb.

Further north the Pennine Way proper leaves the main watershed for the green and rolling hills of Lothersdale. I looked at alternatives in the Ilkley area but the route would have been circuitous. I therefore decided to stick with the original route as far as Lothersdale village but descend to Skipton, where the heather-clad, craggy hills of Embsay Moor and Rylstone Fell provide an excellent alternative to Pinhaw Beacon.

The most extensive changes I made were between Malham and Hawes in the Yorkshire Dales and two days are spent here without the routes converging. Pen y Ghent has been chewed up, mostly by Three Peaks walkers, runners and cyclists, but is nevertheless a prime case for omission. At Malham Tarn my route veers eastwards and heads via Arncliffe for Kettlewell in Wharfedale. An ascent then follows to Buckden Pike, where there is a 360-degree panorama over sev-eral counties of northern England.

North of Keld the Pennine grouse moors are crossed. The terrain becomes bleaker and the hills less shapely. Lovers of solitude will be happier here for these places are quiet. If you do meet somebody chances are they too will be doing the Pennine Way. Options are limited by the lack of access and probably the best route is that of the official way. Nobody could call it over-used in this part of the country.

No Pennine Walk can omit the highest peak, Cross Fell and neither does mine, although an interesting foul weather alternative to Alston via Cow Green is includ-ed. The mountains, which give birth to both the Tyne and Tees rivers, are high, wild and handsome and have been described as England's last wilderness.

Probably one of the least attractive sections of the official route is through the Stonesdale Valley between Alston and Hadrian's Wall. Hereabouts it pussyfoots on the plains and lower slopes of high, heather-clad Pennine hills. For my alternative route I chose the climb over Hard Rigg and Mohope Moor to the lovely valley of the West Allen. This is as beautiful as any Yorkshire Dale and the walk over high pastures, through woodland and by riverbanks is memorable - far superior to the official way!

Wainwright said that the walk should have stopped at Hadrian's Wall. I think he was probably right but the ground rules have already been set. The challenge - and much of the Pennine Way's nature is rooted in challenge - would be diminished by reducing its length and not continuing over the magnificent Cheviot Hills. It is just those in-between bits that irk. For two days the official route messes about in dark spruce plantations punctuated by soggy, shapeless moorland.

Luckily one new development since the inauguration of the 'Way' has been that of the Kielder Reservoir, which opens up new possibilities. My diversion round its shores and on to the crag-fringed heather moors of Kielder Head is a vast improvement on the existing dull plod between Bellingham and Byrness. It also brings the walker to the Cheviot Hills a day earlier, an ideal appetizer for the final day on the high ridges to Kirk Yetholm.

One of the greatest problems in creating new long-distance routes is that of access - or lack of it. The main stumbling block is the grouse-shooting fraternity,

backed by a very high-powered lobby group who, despite concerted efforts by the Ramblers' Association, ensure that vast tracts of our beautiful heather moors are left to those who wish to blow the brains out of defenceless birds. They do it, to use their own words, in the interests of conservation, and frequently inform us that walkers on the land will frighten their birds and disturb their breeding habits (the birds' not the shooters'). The attitude of the landowners is such that Rogan's Seat north of Keld and the High Pennines north of Cross Fell are all out of bounds. Walkers are now more likely than ever to meet an unsympathetic gamekeeper who will turn them back.

The 'no go' areas of the Ministry of Defence have also reduced the options. Noble Mickle Fell, County Durham's highest mountain, would have made an excellent preamble to the traverse of Cross Fell - demanding but so rewarding. Firing ranges in the Otterburn and Cheviot areas restrict routes to the extent that few acceptable alternatives to the original line are feasible.

In the main text I have tried to make the various routes converge at convenient 'valley' centres. The lack of access to the northern moors of the Yorkshire Dales between Hawes and Tan Hill made it difficult to plan a

Wain Wath Force at Keld.

'legal' alternative. I had intended my route to go over Lovely Seat and Rogan's Seat but this would involve walkers in confrontations with the landowners. Further east the situation improves. I decided to offer an East Dales Loop route from Kettlewell to Bowes, which, although well away from the main Pennine watershed, still retains the mountain-walking theme of the 'Way'. It is a superb route which diverts from the Pennine Way valley centres for three days, visiting Buckden Pike, Aysgarth, Reeth and the moors north of Gunnerside.

Whilst I have been writing *Pennine Ways* another long-distance route, the Pennine Bridleway, is being devised and an excellent book, *The Alternative Pennine Way,* has been written. The former route, backed by the Countryside Commission, worries me. I can imagine the route, wherever it may go, being ground into the face of the Pennine Hills by the pounding of horses' hooves and the tyre-marks of mountain bikes. The latter is a pleasant route between Ashbourne and Jedburgh and "not always seeking the high hills". As such it sits well alongside my book. Indeed it could be used in combination with my routes and the official way.

Whichever way you walk it, the Pennine Way will be a major experience. It is one of the world's great trails and traverses unique wild upland. Like all good long-distance routes there is a definite objective - to walk the backbone of England. The hills may not be as high or grand as those of the Lake District or Scotland but they are full of surprises. From the moment you reach the high Kinder Plateau you are aware of the spaciousness of these fells - they offer wide views under wide skies. There is no typical Pennine landscape, for subtle changes occur regularly as the basic rock changes between gritstone, limestone, dolerite and granite. The changes are reflected also in the character of the villages and there are many charming ones just waiting in the valleys to serve the tired walker with a piping hot meal and cool lager.

Do not be overawed by the 250-mile (400km) distance. Although challenging, it is not as tough as its reputation. There is a great camaraderie between 'Pennine Wayers' and you will probably make many new friends. Take each day in isolation and you should soon be celebrating with that free beer in the Border Hotel, Kirk Yetholm, planning next year's walk.

John Gillham, Darwen 1994

The author enjoying a pint at Kirk Yetholm.

1

THE DARK PEAK

Edale to Crowden

The village of Edale sits snugly in its pastoral paradise, surrounded by high peaks. To the south the rounded profiles of Mam Tor and Rushup Edge fall to the River Noe in graceful arcs. On the opposite side of the valley are the castellated gritstone crags which cap the southern face of Kinder Scout. It is in this direction that the Pennine Way walker turns for the first mountain challenge of a formidable 250 mile (400km) trek.

Both official 'Ways' tour the peat-hagged plateaux of Kinder Scout and Bleaklow. The less-favoured Grindsbrook route tackles Kinder more boldly while the more circuitous Jacob's Ladder alternative sticks to the gritstone edges above the pastures of Hayfield and Glossop.

In poor visibility, there is no completely safe traverse of either Kinder or Bleaklow and the ability to use both map and compass is absolutely essential. I have, however, offered a less demanding alternative, taking an easterly course along the high valleysides of Edale before descending to the Derwent Reservoir. The route then utilizes forest tracks by the Derwent and Howden Reservoirs to enter the lonely fells of Howden, where we get a taste of the Dark Peak wilderness before reaching Crowden.

The Upper Derwent Valley from near Broadhead Clough on the alternative route.

EDALE TO CROWDEN
The Official Route via Upper Booth and Jacob's Ladder

A quiet corner of Edale at the start of the walk.

Originally a foul-weather alternative, this is now considered the main Pennine Way route. The various authorities believe that the Grindsbrook route straddling the Kinder Plateau is badly eroded and needs a rest. The change will displease most walkers who will not wish to delay their climb to the mountains. It is, however, a pleasant route, especially above Jacob's Ladder, where firm paths hug the rugged cliff edges.

EDALE
Edale in the early morning is a quiet and charming place and, if you set off on this long journey at this time, you will see it at its best, for the sun's rays give a warm glow to the serrated crags of Grindsbrook on the skyline. A tree-lined track opposite the school sets the course westwards from the village to reach open fields. It continues meekly skirting the slopes of Grindslow Knoll but giving superb views of the beautiful Edale Valley. On the skyline the mountains beckon but on this route we have to wait!

JACOB'S LADDER
After descending to the small farming hamlet of Upper Booth, a narrow metalled lane leads past Lee End Farm, where an old barn is used as a National Trust Information Point. A track then leads to an old packhorse bridge, which is crowded by the steep grassy flanks of Edale Head. A newly renovated path, Jacob's Ladder, climbs boldly to the high ridge at Edale Cross.

At Edale Cross the route strikes northwards over grassy moorland giving good views of Kinder Scout's jagged southern edge. After passing beneath the

Looking east over Edale from Jacob's Ladder, which is the 'stairway' to the Kinder Plateau seen on the official route.

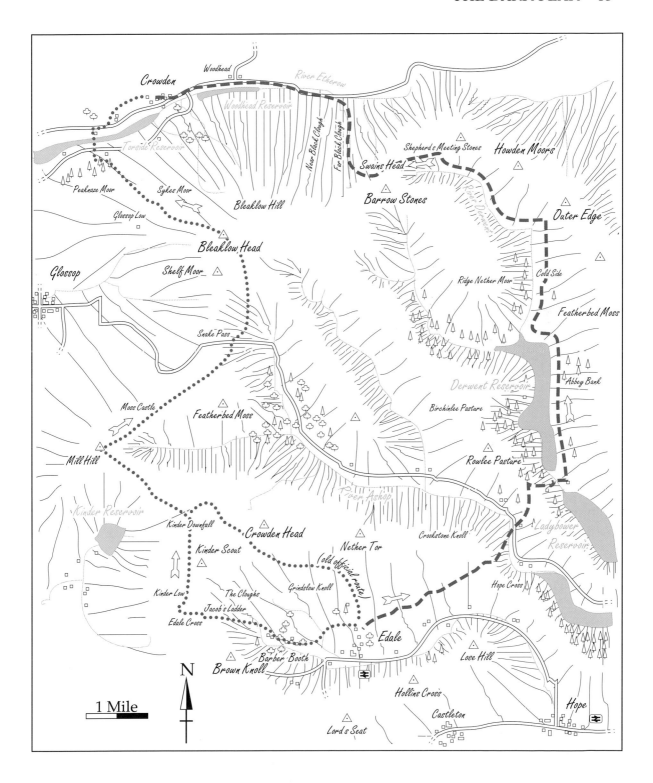

Crowden

Woodhead

River Etherow

Woodhead Reservoir

Torside Reservoir

Peaknaze Moor

Sykes Moor

Glossop Low

Bleaklow Hill

Near Black Clough

Far Black Clough

Swains Head

Shepherd's Meeting Stones

Howden Moors

Barrow Stones

Outer Edge

River Derwent

Bleaklow Head

Shelf Moor

Glossop

Ridge Nether Moor

Cold Side

Featherbed Moss

Snake Pass

Derwent Reservoir

Abbey Bank

Moss Castle

Featherbed Moss

Birchinlee Pasture

Mill Hill

Rowlee Pasture

River Ashop

Kinder Reservoir

Kinder Downfall

Crowden Head

Nether Tor

Crookstone Knoll

Ladybower Reservoir

Kinder Scout

(old official route)

Kinder Low

The Cloughs

Grindslow Knoll

Hope Cross

Jacob's Ladder

Edale Cross

Edale

Barber Booth

Lose Hill

N

Brown Knoll

Hollins Cross

1 Mile

Castleton

Hope

Lord's Seat

Above: The Kinder Downfall. (Photo: Graham Thompson)
Below: The Wain Stones on Bleaklow sneaking their eternal kiss.

gritstone crags of Swine's Back and Edale Rocks the route emerges at Kinder Low's concrete trig. point, which crowns an area of dark peat, lightly sprinkled with gravel and interspersed with boulder and outcrop.

From Kinder Low the way traverses firm ground at the western edge of the plateau. In the western panorama beneath lower, heather-clad hills, is the Kinder Reservoir. Beyond it the industrial plains of Manchester recede to the distant horizon.

Walkers congregate at Bleaklow Head on a crisp winter day.

THE KINDER DOWNFALL

One and a half miles (2.4km) north of Kinder Low the path reaches the Kinder Downfall. After periods of rain this can be a superb spectacle as the waters plummet down a rocky amphitheatre on course for the Kinder Reservoir, seen in the distance amid gentler hills. Alas, most Pennine Way travellers see it in the summer months when it is a mere trickle.

From the downfall, the edge of the plateau is traced to its north-western edge. Unfortunately the joys of walking the firm cliff-top path are foresaken and our route descends steeply to Ashop Head where the famous Snake Path is crossed.

FEATHERBED MOSS

Further ascent is then made on the grassy slopes of Mill Hill, which gives improved views of Bleaklow and also a new aspect - that of Kinder's dark northern crags fringing the aptly named Black Ashop Moor and the desolate valley of Ashop Clough.

The route changes direction on Mill Hill and heads north-east on marshy terrain. The wooden stakes, which act as a guide in poor conditions, cease on the peat hags of Featherbed Moss, a horrid barrier to progress. The busy metalled Manchester to Sheffield highway lies tantalisingly within sight across Holden Clough but there remains a mile of this awful terrain outstanding with no prospect of escape! You'll just have to slither up and down the myriad slimy channels.

THE SNAKE PASS

Known by most from news reports of road blockages after snowfalls, the Snake Pass really looks the part - high and wild! But for Pennine Way walkers it marks the conquering of Kinder Scout, that first hurdle on the long road to Kirk Yetholm, and is thus a welcome sight.

And so Kinder is left behind: ahead lies Bleaklow, an expansive and even wilder barrier to the promise of civilization and a bed for the night at Crowden. From the road the way goes across rough moorland, passing an old Roman highway known as Doctor's Gate (named after Dr John Talbot of Glossop, a frequent user in the sixteenth century). For those who cannot complete the journey to Crowden in one day, Doctor's Gate offers an interesting descent either to Glossop (west) or to the Snake Inn (east).

BLEAKLOW

Beyond Doctor's Gate a line of posts leads to Devil's Dyke, a straight channel through the peat-hagged terrain. This leads north-eastwards to Alport Low, where another line of posts diverts the route north-westwards towards the highest ground, fording Hern Clough en route. Beyond this small stream with its shallow grassy banks, yet more peat bogs are crossed to reach the Hern Stones, which stand proud on Bleaklow's high plateau. The way now heads northwards to the Wain Stones, two gritstone boulders resembling kissing heads when viewed from the south. The highest point,

Bleaklow Head, marked by a tall post and small stone cairn, lies just a little to the north. It is a great relief to know that all is downhill to Crowden - and it's much drier too! Cairns mark the way off the top and the faint path traverses peatlands to the heathery terrain above Wild Boar Grain. The small stream is forded close to its confluence with an unnamed stream at GR 081965. From here the craggy and deepening defile is known as Torside Clough.

LONGDENDALE

The path, now distinct, follows the high edge of the clough and gradually, as it veers to the north, the valley of Longdendale is revealed with Black Hill's southern flanks filling the skyline above the Torside Reservoir. The final descent is on precipitous grassy slopes that terminate at Reaps Farm, whose drive is used to reach the B-road to the south of the reservoir. From here it is obvious that man has done much to disfigure what must once have been a beautiful valley. Running along its length we have two roads, the scarred track of a disused railway, a chain of huge electricity pylons and five reservoirs. Much as we disapprove, most of the developments have been necessary in order for us to live our 'comfortable twentieth-century lives'. Never mind, we are down and can look forward to a good rest at the Youth Hostel or camp-site.

EDALE TO KINDER DOWNFALL
The Old 'Official Route' via Grindsbrook

EDALE

A tarmac lane leads northwards from the Old Nag's Head Inn until a signpost points the way across a wooden footbridge spanning the narrow stream of Grinds Brook. From here a path climbs across green meadows northwards above the brook. As it nears the mountains the path becomes rougher and the scenery more wild. The vale narrows, crowded by the rugged and strangely gnarled cliffs of Upper Tor, Nether Tor and Ringing Roger. The brook is now more boisterous and rushes over its rocky bed in a series of falls and cataracts. On the final stretch to the edge of Kinder's plateau you have to clamber over the rocks. Superb retrospective views include Rushup Edge and Mam Tor across the jagged spurs of Grindslow Knoll and Ringing Roger. These are enhanced in August when

purple patches of flowering heather add further colour to the impressive scenes.

THE KINDER PLATEAU

On reaching the plateau, a wide track leads along the edge westwards to the head of Crowden Clough. On the opposite side of the depression is the impressive gritstone outcrop of Crowden Tower. Many walkers will, from here, be heading north-westwards on the old Pennine Way route across trackless terrain - a vast

The Kinder Gates. Gritstone tors surround the sandy bed of the River Kinder, whose waters are more often than not absent.

undulating expanse of peat-hagged moorland, partially cloaked by cotton sedge, bilberry and heather. To some this is uninviting, especially after the promising crag scenery of Grindsbrook, but to the many devotees of this area it is part of Kinder's rugged appeal.

If you have made an early morning start these moors will be beautifully quiet, except for the sound of the curlew, meadow pipit or the occasional cackle of a disturbed grouse, and to me this tranquillity is part of their intrinsic appeal. After traversing a mile of this rough plateau, the Kinder Gates are reached. Here dark gritstone crags line the reddish sandy beds of the infant River Kinder, which is sometimes a trickle but often dry. The firm bed makes a good path and leads to the plateau's western edge at the Kinder Downfall, where the Jacob's Ladder route is joined.

NB A superior route from the top of Grindslow Brook follows the firmer track along the southern edge of the plateau, passing Crowden Tower and Kinder Low.

This gives better views of the valleys and crags to the south and west and offers a free-striding promenade amongst craggy terrain rather than a moorland trudge in gooey peat.

It would also be feasible to leave the path in Grindsbrook to climb Ringing Roger and Nether Tor. Here the plateau is at its narrowest and a short trek - a quarter of a mile - would lead to the northern edge overlooking the Woodlands Valley. The northern edge could then be traced to meet the main route near Ashop Head. For the Peak District this would be a pleasantly quiet section.

EDALE TO CROWDEN
An Alternative Route via the Derwent Reservoir

My alternative route is ideal during foul weather as it follows the more gentle terrain of Edale's northern hill-slopes into the regions of the Derwent Reservoirs before sampling the wild moors of the Dark Peak at Swains Head. It should be noted that the access area crossed between Swain Head and Longdendale is subject to closure for a few days per year for grouse shooting (see the route file at the end of the chapter).

EDALE
In its initial stages the path gives some of the finest views of Edale, illustrating the graceful contours of the verdant lower slopes and the bold southern ridge at Lose Hill, Mam Tor and Rushup Edge. The River Noe rustles through the valley bottom, its chattering drowned for brief moments by the rumblings of hurrying Manchester to Sheffield 'Sprinter' trains.

From the Nag's Head, a narrow lane leads eastwards to an old pack-horse bridge where a small stream, shaded by trees, is crossed. The route follows an old jaggers' track which formerly linked Edale with Derwent Village. (A jagger was a man who led pack-horses laden with goods across the hills.) The well-defined path continues across high but lush meadowland to the farming hamlet of Ollerbrook Booth. Frequent signs point to courtesy paths which climb to open fells but our path traverses the hillsides, passing Rowland Cote Youth Hostel, pleasantly situated among mixed woodland by Lady Booth Brook.

A mile further east, the path descends to Jaggers Clough before climbing once more to high pastureland on a hill which separates Edale from the Woodlands Valley. The view southwards has widened and includes limestone hills beyond Edale and the belching chimneys of the cement works at a place aptly named Hope.

THE WOODLANDS VALLEY
At GR 163882, the path enters a forest and descends amongst spruce and fir to the Woodlands Valley. The River Ashop is crossed at Haggwater Bridge (163885) and from here we climb through pleasant mixed

The Ladybower Reservoir and the Woodlands Valley from the alternative route on Crookstone Hill.

Approaching Stainery Clough in the Upper Derwent Valley beyond the last reservoir. From here the alternative route climbs to the moors.

woodland to the A57 'Snake Road'. Immediately opposite, a track ascends out of the valley to the east of Hagg Farm, which used to be a youth hostel and camp-site, but is now an outdoor activity centre with no facilities for the hiker. The upper slopes are scaled in zigzags before skirting the Hagg Side Conifer Plantations to another outdoor activity centre at Lockerbrook Farm.

A short distance north of the farm, a Forestry. Commission courtesy path signposted 'To Fairholmes', is used to descend to their visitor centre lying between the Derwent and Ladybower Reservoirs. In summer and on Bank Holidays the centre teems with tourists and is not a place to dwell unless you need refreshments - better to press on along the road, which rounds Ladybower's northern shores!

THE DERWENT RESERVOIRS

To the east of the apex of the bend, the road is abandoned for a footpath which climbs

through the forest to the eastern edge of the Derwent Reservoir's huge dam. From here a track leads northwards by the reservoir's eastern shores. The lake is lined by beautiful woodlands, which cloak the lower slopes of the steep-sided moors.

The track deviates to cross the wild clough of Abbey Brook close to the Howden Dam. Retrospective views from here southwards across the glistening Derwent are quite stunning. The track continues above the sinu-

Looking back across the Upper Derwent Valley from the Shepherds' Meeting Stones.

THE DERWENT RESERVOIRS

Before flooding the Upper Derwent was a long, narrow valley supporting many remote farms. Inhabitants scratched a living from the narrow swathe of fertile land, and also the high barren moors.

At the turn of the century the Derwent Water Board decided to create two reservoirs - the Howden and the Derwent. They built a railway from the main Manchester to Sheffield line close to Bamford, terminating just short of the site of the Howden Dam. This was used to convey hard gritstone rocks and other materials necessary for the ambitious project. A temporary village, Tin Town, was constructed to house the workers and this was sited at the foot of Birchinlee Pasture. Remains of this site can still be seen among the thick forestry for those who wish to explore.

After the completion of the Howden Dam in 1912 and the Derwent Dam in 1916, the waters submerged fourteen farms. Others were later abandoned, having lost their profitable lower fields.

Ladybower, the most southerly of the present reservoirs, was completed in 1946. Two hamlets were decimated in the process - Ashopton and Derwent. The former included a pub and a smithy and the latter a church and village hall. Derwent's pack-horse bridge was reconstructed at Slippery Stones, north of the Howden Reservoir.

ous shorelines of the Howden Reservoir and beyond into the Upper Derwent Valley close to the river at Slippery Stones. Here the original twin-arched bridge that spanned the river at Derwent village has been reconstructed, stone by stone.

THE HOWDEN MOORS

Beyond the bridge the forest is left behind and we enter the wilder environs of the Upper Derwent Valley. The river is lined by scattered oaks and the hills clad with heather and grass close in to form a tight ravine. The track continues over Cranberry Clough and Broadhead Clough. An attractive waterfall cascades down the latter. Beneath the gritstone crags of Crow Stones Edge the valley snakes westwards and the path follows suit. Although more often than not innocuous, the crossing of Stainery Clough can be problematic after heavy rains and it may be necessary in these conditions to climb higher up the valley to make a safe fording. Take care!

Beyond Stainery Clough the woodlands cease. The harsh bare moors, which have taken over, are colourful with heather, bracken and the mottled greens of bilberry and moor grass.

The track ends at a marshy plot beyond Lands Clough. Do not be tempted to follow the path too close to the riverbanks (it's very boggy). Instead use the sketchy course higher up past Humber Knolls and Coldwell Clough.

At GR 144977, a faint path climbs out of the Derwent Valley above the eastern banks of Hoar Clough. On the skyline are a group of rocks known as the Shepherds' Meeting Stones. On reaching them a right of way continues northwards to the main watershed but it is better to head west at this point, crossing the stream and keeping to the gritstone edges, including Dean Head Stones. This way the worst of the marshy peat hags of Featherbed Moss (another one!) can be avoided.

The watershed is met at Swains Head, where a series of stakes guides the walker westwards with drab moorland rising in the distance to the serrated and bouldered top of Bleaklow.

At GR 126982, where the path veers to the south, heading towards Bleaklow Stones, it is abandoned. Our route maintains a westerly direction (trackless) for a couple of hundred yards until we drop into Far Black Clough, a shallow depression hereabouts.

FAR BLACK CLOUGH

The track descending along the eastern banks of Far Black Clough is a clear and well-used one, probably by shooters. The scenery is increasingly pleasant as the clough deepens and becomes fringed with buttresses of millstone grit. The stream transforms from a trickle in the dark peat to a lively watercourse over a rocky bed. The path stays on the eastern edge high above the stream and bordering the heather-clad grouse moors. In the view ahead the miry wilderness that is Black Hill masquerades as a pleasant grassy hill, rising gently from the valley below.

THE WOODHEAD TUNNEL

In the lower regions of the fellside the landscapes soften. Far Black Clough flows into Near Black Clough and the banks are wooded. The clough becomes shallow in the regions of Birchen Bank Wood, a popular

Above: Near Black Clough close to the Woodhead Tunnel.

tourist area close to the A628 road. At GR 117995, by the edge of the wood, the stream is forded using stepping stones. A wide track then follows the stream, which has now become the River Etherow, before recrossing it via a bridge and meeting the busy highway. We are now in Longdendale and the signs of industry past and present are laid before us. Adjacent is the once famous Woodhead Tunnel, which used to convey the Manchester to Sheffield Railway for nearly four miles beneath these high moors. It is now boarded up and redundant.

On the opposite side of the road is a stile, allowing walkers across privately owned access land (by courtesy) to meet the right of way. This gives excellent views of Bleaklow's craggy northern ramparts, which rise beyond the waters of the Woodhead Reservoir. The path leads to Woodhead Bridge, where the road is rejoined.

CROWDEN

After crossing the bridge, there is another courtesy path which wanders the lower fellsides to Crowden Youth Hostel, where we meet the official Pennine Way.

ROUTE FILE

Maps	OS Landranger (1:50000) No.110 'Sheffield' or Outdoor Leisure Map (1:25000) No 1 'Dark Peak'
Distance and time	
via Jacob's Ladder	16 miles (26km) 9 hours
via Grindsbrook	15 miles (24km) 9 hours
via the Derwent Valley	17 miles (27km) 9 hours
Terrain	The peat-hagged plateaux of Kinder and Bleaklow can be very boggy outside the summer months. The paths along Kinder Scout's gritstone edges are good and firm.
Other Notes	Much of Kinder and Bleaklow is covered by an access agreement, which allows freedom to roam. On a few days during the grouse shooting season (12 August to 12 December) and at times of high fire risk the routes not on rights of way will be closed to the public. This includes sections of the alternative route north of the Derwent Reservoirs.
Accommodation	Youth Hostel and camp-site at Crowden.
Shops	Odds and sods at the Youth Hostel shop.
Tourist Information	The Crescent, Buxton, Derbyshire SK17 6BQ. Tel 0298 25106

2

HIGH MOSSES OR THE GRITSTONE EDGE

Crowden to Standedge

More peat, more squelchy marshlands and more wet socks - that is what the second section offers the walker on the official Pennine Way. It is probably the least interesting section of the entire route and the yardsticks of progress are not the mountain-tops but the trans-Pennine roads which parcel the featureless badlands into small sections.

The day begins promisingly in the gorge of the Great Crowden Brook where the Laddow Rocks tower above the wild grasslands. However, as the gorge shallows and narrows to become a dreary moorland clough, the walk deteriorates into a tiresome toil up the featureless slopes of Black Hill whose summit area is blanketed by naked, black, glutinous peat.

At Black Hill another decision has to be made - whether to use the main Pennine Way over White Moss or the official alternative along the Wessenden Valley to the Black Moss Reservoir. The former is one of the badly eroded sections, especially north of the A635, which has become one of the most unsightly morasses on the whole of the route. The choice must be left to your own conscience. Both routes meet once more at Black Moss Reservoir one mile to the south-east of Standedge.

The alternative route I have offered is a much more attractive proposition. It departs from the official line at Laddow Rocks and meets it once more at Standedge Cutting near Diggle. The awful bogs of Black Hill and Wessenden Moor are replaced with an airy walk along the craggy Saddleworth Edges followed by a trek across Alderman's Hill with its intimate views of gritty Pennine villages.

Opposite: The Dean Rocks and Ashway Gap seen on the Dove Stone Edge alternative route.   *Below: Featherbed Moss, Black Hill.*

CROWDEN TO STANDEDGE
The Official Route via Black Hill and the Wessenden Valley

CROWDEN

Black Hill's traitorous bogs loom large in the mind as one sets off from Crowden along the valley of the Crowden Brook. Steps are retraced past the camp-site and rifle range to GR 068991, north of the Torside Reservoir. Here a path through rough grasslands climbs the valley's western flanks below the sullen gritstone cliffs of Black Tor (not marked on 1:50000 maps). Beyond the grassy spur of Bareholme Moss, the Crowden Brook divides to become Crowden Little and Crowden Great Brooks (east and west respectively).

LADDOW ROCKS

A narrow path weaves its way over and around numerous grassy knolls before climbing steeply by the banks of Oakenclough Brook, which is forded to reach the foot of the finest section of gritstone cliffs in the area. These are the Laddow Rocks, a favourite haunt of climbers. Further ascent brings the path to the cliff-top, which is then traced on a well-defined narrow track. A small cairn preceding the highest of the cliffs marks a divergence of paths. Here the official route and my alternative part company. My route (described later), which is easier to follow in the worst mists, takes the left hand path traversing Laddow Moss westwards towards the Saddleworth Edges.

The official Pennine Way continues along the crest of the Laddow Rocks for half a mile before gradually descending to rejoin the lively Crowden Great Brook.

GRAINS MOSS

The quality of the scenery deteriorates as the valley becomes more shallow and the increasingly murky stream is left behind. A sketchy path traverses the drab green moorlands of Grains Moss. Black Hill, in sight ahead, is little more than a mound on the horizon - nothing to fire the imagination, no mountain status - just the anticipated menace of its mires!

BLACK HILL

When the gradient eases to the plateau of Black Hill, the battle commences and soon the Pennine Way walker is faced with terrain which is black, devoid of vegetation and which can be horribly unsure after periods of heavy rainfall. I have to say that in a good summer the summit can be as dry as a bone - a real pussycat in fact! The summit, known as Soldiers Lump, is marked by a pale concrete trig. point perched on a small, firm patch of terrain. In the near future work is planned to restore the footpath and revegetate the area.

The route descends north-eastwards from Black Hill's summit on a cairned course across the bare peat. The situation soon improves and the terrain becomes

The Torside Reservoir, Crowden.

Walking above the Laddow Rocks, north of Crowden.

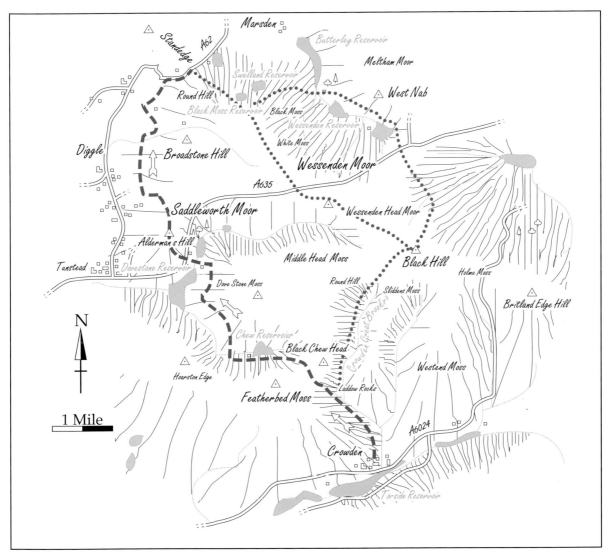

firm once more. The chasm of Issue Clough lends shape to the landscape - something that has been missing since Laddow Rocks. Except in dry spells the waters of the clough cascade between gritstone crags in a spout-like waterfall. Beyond it the more verdant rolling pastures lead the eye to Holmfirth, where scenes from *Last of the Summer Wine* are shot.

As you continue along the cairned path, the views widen and, from this airy stage the cities of Yorkshire are laid before your eyes. The path veers northwards before meeting and following a straight boundary ditch, which straddles the lower moors and three more

cloughs *en route* to the busy A635 road at Wessenden Head. Often there is an ice cream/ hot dog van parked here - a welcome sight for flagging spirits.

THE WESSENDEN VALLEY

The path on the opposite side of the road descends to meet a wide reservoir service road, which in turn descends to the Wessenden Head Reservoir, the most southerly of four which fill this pleasant valley.

The wide track continues northwards to the Wessenden Reservoir, and passes Wessenden Lodge, a stately building which looks as though it has seen better

Above: Descending Black Hill by Issue Clough on the Wessenden route with views across the plains of West Yorkshire.
Below: Blakeley Reservoir from above Blakeley Clough seen on the climb from the Wessenden Valley to Black Moss.

Standedge Cutting and Pule Hill. Underneath the hillsides are three tunnels linking Marsden and Diggle. Two are for the railway. The other is for the canal and is the longest in the country.

days. A notice proclaims that teas are served here, for those in need of refreshment. Opposite is a pleasant waterfall surrounded by thick rhododendron bushes.

BLACK MOSS
To the north of the lodge, the track is abandoned and a Pennine Way sign points the way down to the confluence of Shiny Brook and Blakeley Clough. The former is crossed by a small footbridge and a steep track then climbs the grassy slopes on its opposite banks. After passing a covered water tank, a wide grassy track leads to a weir on Blakeley Clough. The stream is crossed just below the weir and a narrow grooved path continues on the northern bank to the lofty moor of Black Moss. The path becomes more sketchy as it veers right to pass between Swellands and Black Moss Reservoirs. Beyond the latter it turns sharp left and then right on a sandy track across Rocher Moss.

STANDEDGE
From the heather-clad Rocher Moss, the Redbrook Reservoir is sighted with the shapely, crag-fringed Pule Hill behind. The path meets an old pack-horse road, which then descends to the busy A62 west of the reservoir at Standedge. Here a bus service between Oldham and Huddersfield can take the leg-weary to recuperate

in urban civilization. Many Pennine Wayers use the B&B or bunkhouse at nearby Globe Farm.

BLACK HILL TO BLACK MOSS
The Official Alternative via White Moss

Work is being carried out at the time of writing to repair the awful erosion on this section of the route. Although it is the natural ridge route and the most direct it is scenically inferior to the previously described route.

BLACK HILL
In the White Moss route, a north-westerly descent on sketchy paths crosses the green slopes of Wessenden Head Moor which in summer are decorated with the white tufts of cotton grass.

FEATHERBED MOSS AND WHITE MOSS
The A635 Manchester to Huddersfield road is met at GR 052063. Here you will more than likely be greeted by the sight of a white caravan. This is Snoopy's, and the superbly decadent snacks (try the scrumptious sausage, bacon and egg sandwiches and mugs of tea)

served will be most welcome before trudging the moors to the north.

The terrain north of the A635 is horrible! It is a dark and depressing maze of peat hags and is yet another Featherbed Moss. The paths across it are formed by chestnut palings and planks although more permanent constructions are imminent. After plodding for a third of a mile, an overgrown trench of an old road is encountered. This is the Cotton Famine Road, built between Greenfield and Holmfirth to give employment during the cotton famine which brought times of great hardship and suffering to the area.

A cairned track leads north-westwards across White Moss, continuing over the more heathery Black Moss to the dam of the lonely Black Moss Reservoir where it meets the Wessenden Valley route.

LADDOW ROCKS TO STANDEDGE
An Alternative Route via Dovestone Edge

This fine route is aesthetically far superior to the official ways, is far easier to follow in mists, and offers easier escape routes in foul conditions. It also keeps high

enough on the hillsides to keep the Pennine traverse idea intact. In anything other than perfect weather conditions, only lovers of bog and blinkered purists could argue the case for scaling Black Hill.

LADDOW ROCKS
A small cliff-top cairn before the highest of the rocks marks the divergence of paths. The alternative route veers westwards on a reasonably firm, well-defined path across the peat-hagged expanses of Laddow Moss. Once over the top, the cairned track follows the groove of a tiny stream, often dry. From the undulating terrain, fleeting glimpses are caught of England's highest reservoir, Chew Green (1600 ft /490 metres).

The path eventually descends to the reservoir, passing its southern shores on the course of an old railway built to supply men and materials for its construction. This is a popular tourist spot and, at peak times, the loneliness of the surrounding moors will be rudely disturbed.

DOVE STONE EDGE
At the huge earth-fill dam a reservoir supply road is followed down the wild and craggy Chew Valley. The road, which leads eventually down to Greenfield, can be used as an escape route . It is abandoned just short

Dish Stone Brow and the rocky ravine of Chew Brook.

of a disused quarry (GR 034018) for a sketchy track heading westwards. The firmer ground near to the edge is followed, passing numerous strangely-shaped boulders, perched high above the deepening Chew Valley.

Soon the Dove Stone Reservoir comes into view. Beyond it is Alderman Hill, topped by a gritstone-bouldered cap and obelisk. As progress is made northwards-the view opens out to reveal more of the reservoir and also the verdant surroundings of the mills and dwellings of Greenfield. A rather unusual ruin, Bramley's Cot, is passed. This former dwelling was built into a cliff edge and the groove can still be seen where the roof would have been attached. A short distance to the north is the Cairn on Fox Stone, a memorial to two young climbers killed in the Dolomites in 1972.

The Dove Stone Reservoir seen from the track to Alderman Hill.

We now enter the finest stretch of crag scenery of the day. The Great Dove Stone Rocks fringe boulder-strewn flanks, which tumble to the reservoir below. Another reservoir, the Yoeman Hey, is now in view to the north, flanked by a small plantation of conifers, lending a little fresh colour to the scene.

THE ASHWAY GAP

Beyond the Great Dove Stone rocks, the path veers right (east) to cross the Ashway Gap. It is quite a circuitous but unavoidable detour. The stream, Dove Stone Clough, is crossed at GR 032038 by a small cataract and the succeeding path continues at the edge of the moorland to the west of the Ashway Stone. Ahead are the serrated Ashway Rocks and a cross commemorating the death of an MP, killed in a shooting accident.

THE YOEMAN HEY RESERVOIR

A well defined track leaves the plateau's edge and gradually descends beneath the Ashway Rocks. The right of way is shown as zigzagging down to the weirs at the clough bottom but in fact a clear track continues along the grassy flanks to exit on the Water Authority road close to the Yoeman Hey Dam. The dam is crossed and the road continues southwards through conifer plantations. At GR 018043, a signpost points the way to the Binn Green car park, where the A635 road is encountered.

ALDERMAN'S HILL

On the opposite side of the road a cart track, named on the 1:25000 sheets as Long Lane, circumvents the southern slopes of Alderman's Hill before climbing to its summit. The top is crowned by a huge obelisk erected to commemorate the dead of both World Wars. On reading the memorial tablets you cannot help feeling a little sadness for many of the same family names seem to crop up as casualties in both wars. On a clear day you look down on the villages of Saddleworth lying snugly in their narrow green valleys and the troubles of the past seem so far away. But peace is as transient as the seasons and the next generations of these same families could be listed once more on that monument.

After passing through a gateway in the iron railings to the north of the monument, a rutted track leads north-eastwards to Dick Hill. From the top, Black Hill is once more visible as is the tall television mast of Holme Moss. An Oldham Way sign (one of many) then points the way northwards to an outcrop of gritstone crags known as the Shaw Rocks (GR 015056 - which are only named on 1:25000 maps). The hill's western edge is then followed for a third of a mile to another Oldham Way signpost. This 'Way' is once again followed westwards downhill to pick up a farm track. We are now at the edge of a verdant basin surrounded by high moors. Below lies the expanding village of Diggle. To the north, the direction we will eventually follow, the pastures rise to the arcing gritstone crags of Standedge, an outlier of the South Pennine group.

THE OUTSKIRTS OF DIGGLE

At a rightangle bend in the farm track (GR 012063) the route continues, descending across fields by a wall to meet a country lane. A farm track on the opposite side of the lane is then followed for a few steps before turning right (northwards) on a footpath traversing undulating pastures. Another country lane is encountered and here the continuation of the footpath is staggered to the right. A signpost points the way northwards once more on a narrow path through overgrown

shrubs close to a large house. The path continues across fields parallel to the flanks of Broadstone Hill with only one obscure point at a wall corner close to a line of wooden electricity pylons. Here we go through the gate to the left then through another immediately to the right. After scaling a primitive wall stile at the northern end of the next field the way becomes obvious again continuing northwards through gaps in the intervening walls to reach a metalled lane. High on the grassy hillslopes to the right, Ravenstone Rocks overlook an old mill. To the left, by the roadside, is a curious statue with no identifying tablet.

STANDEDGE

After turning left along the lane turn right at the next junction. At the first corner a five-bar gate marks the start of a bridleway (no signpost), which climbs towards a huge stone-built house on the hillslopes to the north west. After passing behind the house, the bridleway rakes up moorland slopes, passing by the air shafts of the Standedge Railway tunnel before reaching the busy A62 road, where the main Pennine Way is rejoined.

Shaw Rocks on Dick Hill, near Diggle looking to Standedge.

OF MIRES AND BOGS

Peat. Since you will be up to your ankles (if you're lucky!) in the stuff you might as well know something about it! The black glutinous substance, which has been formed over several thousand years consists of decaying and compressed vegetation.

Examples of the peat bogs of Kinder Scout and Bleaklow can usually be found by searching the map for the word 'Moss'. In these areas, the poor drainage through the impervious millstone grit resulted in the soils becoming waterlogged and covered with peat-forming sphagnum mosses. Through these grew tufts of deer and cotton sedge, liverworts, bog myrtle and bog asphodel and then the insect-eating sundew. The high acidity of the soils prevented the spread of many other botanical species. When the old vegetation decayed it propagated new layers of peat which supported new growths of vegetation and so the chain continued.

Those who traverse the Dark Peak will notice that the moss cover is now restricted to small patches. It has been replaced by sedges, grasses heather and bilberry in a vegetation cover riven by deep and numerous hags in which the naked peat comes to the surface. The base of the hag has often been eroded to the gravelly surface of the core rocks. There are many reasons for this. The chief factors have been sheep-grazing and the industrial pollution of the last century, which has killed the bog-forming mosses thus breaking the chain.

The effect of drainage, both natural and unnatural has also been a significant factor. Dissection of the peat has occurred naturally when, after the rains, drainage water flows below the ground surface excavating a channel in the process. Eventually the surface peat collapses to form a gulley which spreads, slowly at first, then more rapidly as surrounding peat dries and cracks forming yet more channels. Peat can hold a massive amount of water but occasionally it becomes too saturated and the thin surface vegetation is ripped apart as the bog bursts open. This is known as a bog flow and almost always leaves the surrounding area in a chaotic jumble.

Peat bogs have also been lost as the grouse moors have been extended over the years. This is achieved simply by digging drainage ditches. The land is soon cloaked with heather which prefers the new drier conditions.

The summit of Black Hill, one of the worst examples of erosion in the Peak District.

ROUTE FILE

Maps	OS Landranger (1:50000) No.110 'Sheffield and Huddersfield'		
Distance and time			
Official Route	11 miles (18 km)	7 hours	
via White Moss	9 miles (15 km)	6 hours	
via Dovestone Edge	12 miles (19 km)	7 hours	
Terrain	Black Hill has the worst mires on the whole of the Pennine Way although efforts are being made to improve the paths and reseed the summit area . The boggy theme continues on the White Moss route. The moorland paths of the Wessenden route, once off Black Hill, are much firmer. Good paths abound on the grit stone edges of the Dove Stone alternative.		
Accommodation	Camp-site and Bunkhouse at Globe Farm. More available at Diggle and Marsden.		
Shops	None on the route. Some at Diggle and Marsden		
Tourist Information	Station Forecourt, Norfolk Street, Glossop, Derbyshire SK13 8BS. (Tel. 04574 5920)		

— 3 —

TRAVERSE OF THE SOUTH PENNINES

Standedge to the Calder Valley

In the region of Standedge the spreading conurbations of Manchester and Huddersfield crowd the Pennines, which are at their narrowest. To leave the line of the official Pennine Way here would be to leave the hilltops themselves. As a result my alternatives do not begin until Blackstone Edge, where the range broadens to take in the West Pennine Moors and the Forest of Rossendale. After an interesting stroll along boulder-strewn cliff-tops, the walk degenerates reaching an all-time low in the dark swampy peat-hags of Redmires.

Fortunately the short climb to Blackstone Edge heralds a change to the firmer terrain and brighter prospects, which are perpetuated at the next peak, Stoodley Pike.

My alternative route explores the higher, windswept moors to the west of Stoodley Pike. It is splendid country for those who are confident with map and compass but perhaps not for novices, who may find it difficult to locate the faint tracks and complex ridges. Both routes decline to the Calder Valley, a strange juxtaposition of rural charm and industrial heritage.

Opposite: Approaching the monument on Stoodley Pike.

Below: On the summit rocks of Blackstone Edge.

STANDEDGE TO THE CALDER VALLEY
The Official Route

MILLSTONE EDGE

A cart track leads from the busy A62 at Standedge across rough pastures on an easy gradient until it reaches a signposted path climbing northwards to Millstone Edge. Here the high moors of reddish peat end abruptly at the 'edge', which is more akin to a chaotic jumble of boulders. The western flanks decline to the valley of the Upper Tame where small towns such as Diggle and Greenfield hug the barren sides of Saddleworth Moor.

Near to the summit trig. point of Millstone Edge is the Ammon Wrigley memorial stone. Ammon Wrigley (1861-1946) was a poet from Saddleworth whose joy in these high places was illustrated in many of his works. A firm sandy path continues in a delightful promenade to Northern Rotcher, the escarpment's last rock outcrop. It then traverses the rough grass and heather of Oldgate Moss to reach yet another trans-Pennine road, the A640 between Rochdale and Huddersfield.

WHITE HILL

After passing over Rapes Hill, the huge Windy Hill GPO mast comes into view in the middle distance. There is a slight depression to Readycon Dean where there are downstream views of its reservoir.

The summit of White Hill is firm and grassy, a change from its marshy surroundings. From here the path goes westwards to the gravelly terrain of Axletree Edge (not marked on 1:50000 OS maps) where it veers north, descending to the A672. The busy M62 motorway can be seen crossing the high moors and the drone of speeding motorcars may be heard above the whisper of the mountain breeze.

Across the A672 the Windy Hill station is passed. The height of its mast is better appreciated from close proximity. A brief descent follows to the motorway, where a narrow concrete footbridge conveys the walker high above the noisy thoroughfare. (Alterations to this course may be necessary when the motorway's planned widening takes place.)

BLACKSTONE EDGE

Beyond the motorway, a cart track leads north-west-wards to the aptly named Slippery Moss. This is followed by the depressing dankness of the infamous Redmires, once described as the worst mile of the Pennine Way. Even after the slight improvements (palings, planks and primitive bridges over oozing peat) this must rank pretty highly in the list of places in which not to dwell. To the north-west lies Green Withens Reservoir, doing its best to enliven a desolate landscape.

The depressing scenes do not last long, however and, as the climb to Blackstone Edge nears the ridge, the hags disappear to be replaced by firmer peat which is in turn broken up by spasmodic gritstone boulders amongst the heather and coarse grasses. The summit itself is a magnificent one, being laden with shapely outcrops of millstone grit, some darkened by the stains of bygone heavy industries. From the trig. point,

On the Millstone Edge near Standedge, looking back to Diggle and the Tame Valley.

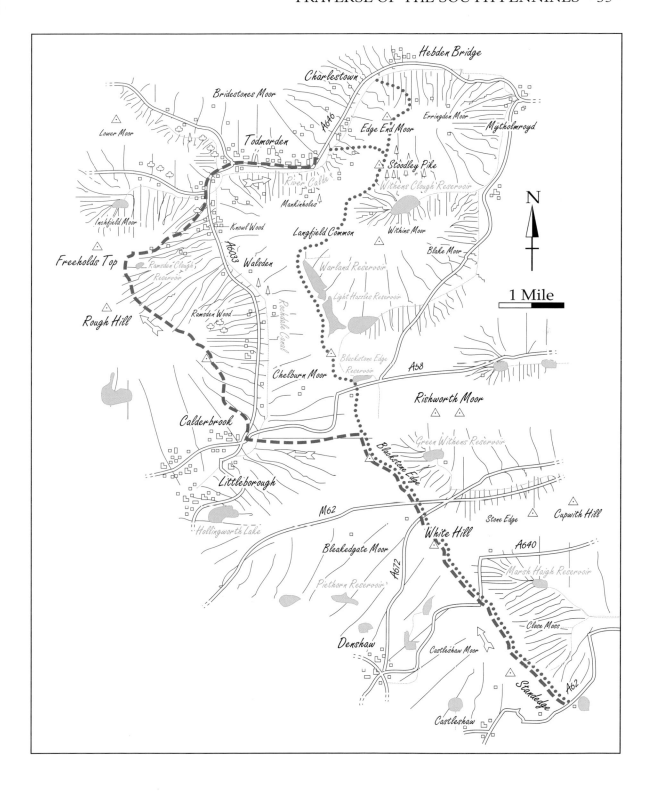

Above: On the summit of Blackstone Edge with Hollingworth Lake framed by the huge boulders.
Below: The well-preserved flagstones of the old Blackstone Edge Roman Road with Littleborough in the valley below.

Walking on the track beside the Warland Reservoir south of Todmorden - one of the fastest and easiest sections of the Pennine Way.

perched on one of these outcrops, there are panoramic views over the plains of Manchester, including the circular Hollingworth Lake, often adorned with the brightly coloured sails of small racing yachts. Blackstone Edge was described as 'the Andes of the north' by *Robinson Crusoe* author, Daniel Defoe, and although one cannot quite match his enthusiasm for the place, it feels good to be here after the hardships of the day.

A pleasant path descends northwards for half a mile to the Aiggin Stone (an old guide post), where it meets the famous Blackstone Edge Roman road. Most historians believe the well preserved flagstones belong to the era before the industrial revolution, when similar pack-horse roads were profuse. Few doubt, however, that this was once the course of a Roman road.

THE WHITE HOUSE INN

The official Pennine Way goes directly north-west over the moors to meet the A58 highway by the Blackstone Edge Reservoir but most travellers descend the Roman Road to the Broad Head Drain (a water company leat), which is then followed northwards. Both meet the A58 by the White House Inn (GR 968178). (NB My alternative route, described later in the chapter, continues its descent along the Roman Road to Littleborough.)

Beyond the inn, a flat-surfaced Water Board road meanders past three large reservoirs (the Blackstone Edge, Light Hazzles and Warland), high on the edge

of a vast tract of heather-clad moorland. The gravelled road allows fast and easy progress. When my nephew (author Roy Clayton) and I did the Pennine Way, we walked this section in the twilight after supper at the White House - Cumberland sausage and chips washed down with cool lager. It was a memorable walk with the lights of Rochdale and Littleborough illuminating the valley below, and the dark outlines of Shore and Inchfield Moors fading into inky skies. We pitched our tent in the heather of Langfield Common at the north end of Warland Reservoir but I cannot recommend this for it contravenes the Water Company's rules.

Beyond the reservoirs, the way follows the line of the Warland Drain, a leat which collects waters from the numerous moorland streams. The leat is left at GR 965220 where a well-defined path strikes northwards for Coldwell Hill. By this time the huge obelisk crowning Stoodley Pike can be seen on the northern skyline. From Coldwell Hill's summit, the first views of the Calder Valley and the craggy north-western slopes of the moors are seen to good advantage. The greenness of the patchwork fields, the urban sprawl of Todmorden and the rough moorlands of Heptonstall beyond all add to a curious marriage of contrasting landscapes.

At Withens Gate (368 spot height on 1:50000 OS maps), a path consisting of weather-smoothed flagstones leaves the hillsides for Mankinholes Youth Hostel and camp-site. This can be used by those who want to call it a day. It is a short and relatively effort-

Stoodley Pike seen from Withens Gate above Mankinholes.

less walk to regain the craggy ridge on the next morning.

STOODLEY PIKE

Some will want to continue along the official line to the Calder Valley at Charlestown, situated between Todmorden and Hebden Bridge. They will follow the sandy path on the escarpment's edge to Stoodley Pike.

The grimy 120ft monument crowning this noble hill has a history of collapses. It was first built in 1815 after three locals, Tom Sutcliffe, Sam Greenwood and Bill Ingham met at the Golden Lion Inn, Todmorden and decided to commemorate the Peace of Ghent and Napoleon Bonaparte's abdication. They were granted the present plot from the Langfield Estate and duly erected their monument, which resembled a mill chimney. Unfortunately it collapsed on 8 February 1854, the day that the Russian Ambassador left London at the start of the Crimean War.

Two years later, after another meeting in the Golden Lion, the lads rallied local people, who then raised the necessary funds to build the obelisk-shaped monument much as it appears today. A rebuild was again necessary after a partial collapse in November 1918, just after peace was declared in the First World War.

Those wishing to enter the monument can do so from the north side. A spiral staircase with forty steps leads eerily into the complete darkness of the inner

recesses before emerging onto the viewing platform. From here are uninterrupted views of Calderdale and south-east Lancashire. The surrounding hills are smooth-profiled and green and from this vantage they give no impression of their inherent roughness. Todmorden below looks as clean as a whistle and fresh colour is added by the red-tiled roofs of its newer dwellings. A far cry from its grimy industrial roots.

For those who wish to undertake my alternative route across Black Hameldon (outlined in the next chapter) a descent could be made westwards via the hospital, crossing the River Calder at GR 960247. The official line from the Pike, however is eastwards to a dry-stone wall (GR 978243), beyond which it veers north-north-east, descending high pastures to Lower Rough Head Farm (GR 981254). Here a cart track leads to Callis Wood (unnamed on (1:50000 maps).

CHARLESTOWN

The track zigzags through shady woods to the industrial surroundings of the Calder Valley. The buzz of the road and railway can be heard through the trees. Rows of terraced houses appear on the far side of the valley, clinging to steep tree-clad hillsides. The canal is crossed: it is often decorated with highly coloured barges, and (unfortunately) a sewage works, passed on

the way to the road. A frequent bus service runs between Todmorden and Hebden Bridge for those who seek hotel or guest-house accommodation. The latter is a fine Yorkshire town of staunch character, built from the local gritstone at the meeting place of four sylvan vales (deans).

BLACKSTONE EDGE TO TODMORDEN
Alternative Route via Crook Moor

This wild moorland route is only recommended in reasonable weather for, if the mist is down, route-finding over featureless moors would be extremely difficult. It is worth noting that the open moorland to the north of the Watergrove Reservoir belongs to North West Water and you are free to roam. On a good day you could simply head for the high ridges and summits west of Great Hill.

BLACKSTONE EDGE
The route begins with the descent of the Roman road to reach the B-road at Lydgate, which is followed for half a mile to GR 945167 on the outskirts of Littleborough. A signposted bridleway then leads to the busy A58.

LITTLEBOROUGH (GALE)
On the opposite side of the road a footpath continues down to the Rochdale Canal, which is crossed via a single-arched stone bridge. A winding path then leads to the Todmorden Road close to the Gale Inn (B&B).

A return to the moors now begins on a signposted route, climbing through a copse of sycamore to some grassed-over quarries high above the sports fields of Littleborough. Where the footpath divides, take the right fork and the course leads above woodlands and across fields to a high country lane between the villages of Shore and Summit. We are now on a high shelf of pastureland, punctuated by farms and cottages, built with the millstone grit hewn from the hillsides.

SHORE MOOR
After turning right along the lane for a short distance it is abandoned for a farm track, which heads northwestwards. At its termination a right turn is made to Far Hey Head Farm, where a left turn is made to follow a stony track to the open moorland at Ringing Pots Hill. A grassy, rutted track to the right is then followed. It climbs northwards above a wild clough (unnamed

On Crook Hill, one of the wild moors seen on the alternative route.

on the maps). After reaching an expanse of bracken (kept to the right) the sketchy path climbs towards the ridge, becomes non-existent for a while and then resumes as a faint groove heading westwards through sparse, grassy moorland south of the highest ground. The path briefly fades into obscurity amongst reeds and sphagnum moss but the groove of its course can be clearly seen climbing the rough hill slopes beyond.

CROOK HILL

The path veers southwards to cross a stream by a stone cairn but then diverts north-westwards to climb to Crook Hill, whose top is crowned by a small pile of stones. The views have opened up southwards to reach panoramic proportions and now include the expansive Watergrove Reservoir, set in a wide bowl of high pastures, and the vast plains and cityscapes of Greater Manchester. Completed in 1938 the reservoir now obscures the ruins of Watergrove village, whose two cotton mills once thrived with the impetus of the industrial revolution. Now there are usually speed-boats and yachts scurrying across its waters. The rounded, barren hill slopes are slightly scarred by the spoil from coal pits, which once formed an important part of the local economy and fired the neighbouring steam-powered mills.

ROUGH HILL

The route continues in a north-westerly descent on a grassy track down to a wide moorland pass. After crossing Higher Slack Brook, a feeder stream of the Watergrove Reservoir, our route climbs northwards to reach the ridge to the east of the summit of Rough Hill. To the north, the bare grassy escarpment of Inchfield Moor dominates the landscape.

RAMSDEN CLOUGH

The path now traverses Rough Hill's northern slopes before descending by an unnamed small stream to meet Ramsden Clough, which is forded at GR 910209, to the south-west of its reservoir. After climbing the northern banks, the path crosses into a field via a small ladder stile, and heads in the direction of a large ruin, Coolam (not named on 1:50000 maps). It then veers north-eastwards on a reedy track, passing more ruins high above the Ramsden Clough Reservoir.

After passing under electricity pylons the track veers to the right and it is abandoned to cross east-north-east over the Inchfield Pasture (also not named

on 1:50000 maps). This high moorland plateau to the east of Inchfield's two reservoirs is covered with cotton-grass. To the north the bare heights of Black Hameldon overlook the hamlets of Cross Stone and Hole Bottoms, which lie on a verdant shelf, high above the chequered fields of the Calder Valley.

TODMORDEN

At GR 923223, just before a stream crossing, an old track, paved in places by slabs of millstone grit, is followed across lofty fields before meeting a farm track. As it descends the valleysides, the houses, factories, viaducts, railway and canal of Todmorden gradually appear in a fascinating tapestry of rural and urban landscape.

Beyond the last farm, Hollow Dene, a narrow tarmac lane descends in zigzags, emerging from behind an old mill and tall brick chimney to the Bacup Road. The road leads down to the banks of the Rochdale Canal, whose towpath leads us by factories and terraces to the bustling market town of Todmorden.

ROUTE FILE		
Maps	OS Landranger (1:50000) Nos.110 'Sheffield', 109 'Manchester' and 103 'Blackburn & Burnley'. Outdoor Leisure Map 21 'South Pennines' would be useful.	
Distance and time Official Route to Charlestown	14 miles (22km)	8 hours
Alternative route to Todmorden	15 miles (24km)	9 hours
Terrain	More peat moors are traversed but, with the exception of Redmires, none are as bad as Black Hill or Bleaklow. On the official route the going is very easy from Blackstone Edge onwards. The alternative has to reascend on rough, grassy moorland after descending to the valley at Littleborough.	
Accommodation	The White House Inn, Blackstone Edge; youth hostel at Mankinholes (above Todmorden). Plentiful accommodation at Todmorden and Hebden Bridge.	
Shops	At Todmorden, and Hebden Bridge. Store at Mankinholes Youth Hostel. Supplies will be available at High Gate Farm, Blackshaw Head encountered early on the next section on the official route. Also available at Littleborough on the alternative route.	
Tourist Information	1 Bridge Gate, Hebden Bridge, West Yorkshire HX7 8EX. Tel. 0422 843831.	

— 4 —

EXPLORING BRONTÉ COUNTRY
The Calder Valley to Lothersdale

The quagmires of the Dark Peak have long been left behind. The official Pennine Way begins the day with a steep climb out of the Calder Valley to cross high farmlands before traversing Heptonstall Moor and Withens Height. The area is in the heart of Bronté Country - bleak moors studded with lonely reservoirs contrast with pleasant valleys.

On descending to the old mill town of Cowling we cross the frontiers of a new landscape between the high gritstone hills of the South Pennines and the limestone bastions of the Yorkshire Dales. It is rolling and verdant countryside with a complex system of valleys, winding country lanes and hidden hamlets. Lothersdale, which lies in one of these tranquil valleys, is an ideal resting place at the end of the day.

My alternative route climbs to the top of Black Hameldon and Boulsworth Hill. It is a bolder, longer and more arduous route but efforts are repaid in full with superb panoramas from the finest summits in the South Pennines. It is a must for those who want to keep to the highest land and it will retain the purist ideal of 'walking the Pennine Ridge'.

On the summit of Boulsworth Hill, highest of the South Pennine peaks. It is seen on the alternative route.

THE CALDER VALLEY TO LOTHERSDALE
The Official Route via Withins Height

CHARLESTOWN

It is a steep climb out of the Calder Valley and one that gives little respite until the high lane to Blackshaw Head is attained. A deviously meandering route leaves the A646 road on a small side road (Underbank Avenue, GR 972265) passing under a railway bridge. A paved footpath winds between a few picturesque cottages and then by the ruins of an old Baptist chapel. The retrospective view includes Stoodley Pike, towering above the busy Calder Valley where Charlestown's stone-built mills shelter beneath the woods and fields of the lower slopes.

BLACKSHAW HEAD

Beyond the chapel there are two possible routes: the official one and Wainwright's. As Wainwright's is the more direct I will describe his version. The path turns sharp right across moorland to reach a cart track to Dew Scout Farm (not named on the maps). To the north a right (east) turn is made along another farm road before turning left (north) across fields, passing Popples and Scammerton Farms. Beyond them we reach the road east of Blackshaw Head at GR 967274.

COLDEN WATER

The route continues to the top of Pry Hill (only named on 1:25000 maps) before descending to Colden Water, a clear watercourse flowing through a pleasant wooded dell. Massive gritstone boulders and slabs line the riverbank and afford the tired walker a seat from which to dangle and revive aching feet in the refreshing waters of the stream.

After crossing Colden Water via the stone bridge and scaling its opposite banks, the path climbs north on a walled farm track before reaching the hamlet of Colden on the Blackshaw Head-Heptonstall road. It continues northwards to reach a narrow metalled farm lane (GR 966287). Although off-route it is worth noting that High Gate Farm, one hundred yards to the west along this lane, sells a wide range of products including food, fuel for camping stoves, maps, drinks (alcoholic and non-alcoholic), even tent pegs and saucepans. They keep a register of signatures of the

Todmorden and the industrial environs of the Calder Valley from the east. Cross Stone church is seen to the right on the horizon.

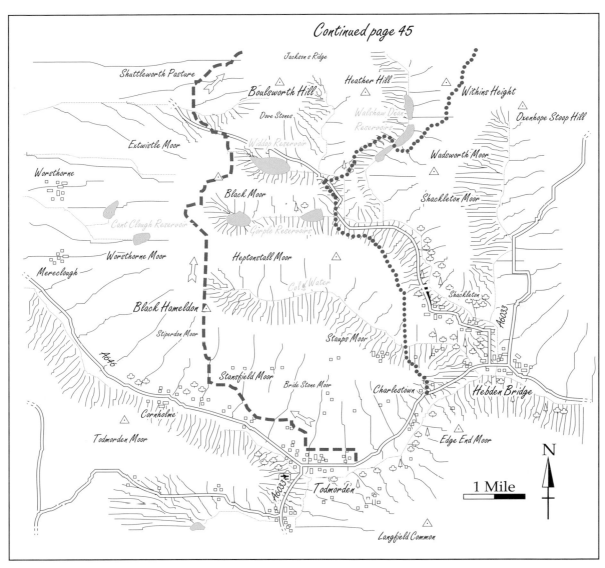

Continued page 45

Pennine Way walkers and take a keen interest in the route. Camping is also available and you can get a cup of tea here.

HEPTONSTALL MOOR

The walled path from the lane climbs northwards past Long High Top and Mount Pleasant Farms to reach the wild open spaces of Heptonstall Moor. We are in true Pennine hill country once more! Beyond Clough Head (GR 962297), where there are glimpses of the valley of Hebden Water, a north-westerly course, veer-ing west, traverses rough grassy hillsides. On the high-est ground retrospective views include Stoodley Pike while, to the north, the lonely Gorple Reservoirs shelter in the aptly named sullen slopes of Black Moor. The eye is led to a remote, white-washed building on a hill to the east of the reservoirs. This is the Pack-Horse Inn, which is regularly isolated by the snow storms each winter. The highest peak on the northern horizon is Boulsworth Hill.

After joining a track which descends to the east of the Lower Gorple Reservoir's dam, the path descends

Dusk descends over the Walshaw Dean Reservoirs in the heart of Bronté country.

by two cottages to reach the charming miniature land-scape of Graining Water. The busy stream snakes between the gritstone cliffs and bluffs crowding its bracken-clad banks. Two wooden footbridges are used to cross firstly a tributary and then Graining Water itself. A narrow path, paved in places, then climbs to the Colne to Hebden Bridge Lane a third of a mile from the Pack-Horse Inn.

WALSHAW DEAN RESERVOIRS

The lane is followed north-westwards to GR 947324. Here a metalled Water Board road allows speedy progress down Walshaw Dean, which has been flooded to form three elongated reservoirs. The Pennine Way crosses the dam of the middle reservoir and follows its eastern shores by rhododendron bushes, which seem more alien to the stark moorland surroundings than the reservoirs themselves.

WITHINS HEIGHT

Shortly after crossing Black Clough, the path climbs north-eastwards to the open heather-cloaked hill slopes of Withins Height. From the top of this peaty hill we can survey Bronté country. To the north, the pale grassy hills undulate and descend to the pastures of the Worth Valley. Beyond the mass of Boulsworth Hill lies the unmistakable escarpment of Pendle Hill, famous for its association with witchcraft.

The descent is made northwards, passing the deso-late and windswept ruins of Top Withins, whose gnarled and twisted attendant trees add to a mysterious and romantic setting. A plaque erected on its wall by the Bronté Society reads:

This farm-house has been associated with 'Wuthering Heights', the Earnshaw home in Emily Bronté's novel. The buildings, even when com-plete, bore no resemblance to the house she described but the situation may have been in her mind when she wrote of the moorland setting of the Heights.

I like to think that this was indeed the house and many unaccustomed pilgrims who hike from Haworth to see it will agree!

THE WORTH VALLEY

After circumventing the head of South Dean a farm track is followed along a spur known as The Height. This passes several farms before we turn left for a lane descending northwards to Buckley Farm and thence to the dam on the eastern end of Ponden Reservoir. A lane then goes left near to the reservoir's shores, passing Ponden Hall, almost certainly 'Thrushcroft Grange' from *Wuthering Heights*. The well preserved building has a stately presence that contrasts with the spartan hill farms higher up the hillsides. Refreshments are provided here for the dishevelled Pennine Way walker!

The Colne to Stanbury road is met by the western extremity of the lake. After a left turn along it, an ascent is made over the steep meadows of Dean Fields before skirting the woods of Crag Bottom to meet the high and winding Oakworth Lane. From here there are good retrospective views across the Worth Valley. Ponden Reservoir lies in rich farmlands. Dry-stone walls contour gently the lower valley-sides to the edge of the moors where the drab hues of the mountain grasses continue to the skyline. The craggy combe of Ponden Clough is seen at its best and the high and isolated Top Withens is just discernible.

WOLF STONES

The lane is followed past some rustic stone-built terraced cottages to GR 985378, where a rough walled track climbs past a badly-sited rubbish tip. A reedy

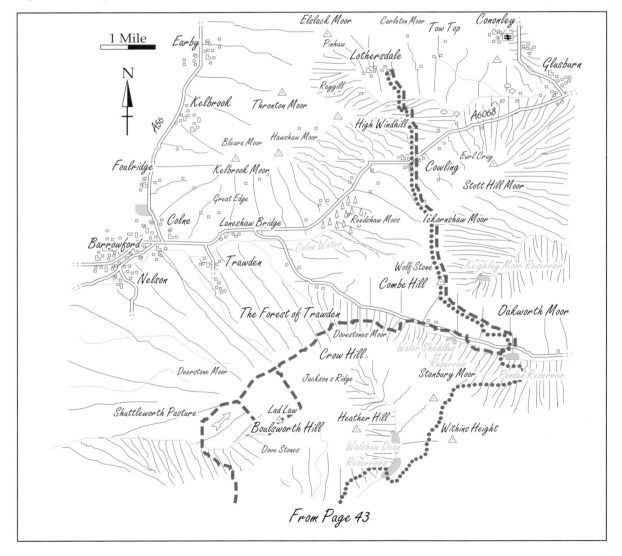

From Page 43

Top Withins. Was this the Wuthering Heights from Emily Brontë's novel.

across Ickornshaw Moor. Ruined farm dwellings are circumvented before meeting a farm track crossing Lumb Head Beck just to the east of its waterfalls. Looking eastwards down the beck, which is tightly enclosed by high grassy slopes, the attention is caught by an obelisk on a nearby shapely hill. Known as Wainman's Pinnacle (and well worthy of a sight-seeing detour), it stands on the edge of Earl's Crag, affording wonderful views on all but the southern horizon. Another monument, Lund's tower, lies on the far side of the crag but is obscured from this vantage.

path by a tall stone wall is then followed north-west-wards over rough grasslands interspersed with clumps of heather and bilberry. The wall terminates on the curiously named Old Bess Hill and soon the squarish profile of the Great Wolf Stones comes into view on the western edge of the moor.

A cairned track then traverses a marshy area of heather-clad peat. Duck-boards are strategically placed over the worst spots. At Bare Hill the track veers to the right away from the Wolf Stones - those who want to see them will have to make a short detour westwards from the ridge (an easy stroll across short heather). The views from these huge gritstone crags are good and worth the small effort. The dominant and angular peak to the south is Boulsworth Hill. It rises from the high pass cradling the lonely Water Sheddles Reservoir. To the west, across the plains of East Lancashire, is the lone escarpment of Pendle Hill while, in the opposite direction, the beautiful Worth Valley meanders to the distant village of Haworth. It is the view to the north, however, that gladdens the heart. If atmospheric conditions are clear, the pale outlines of the peaks of the Yorkshire Dales (including Pen-y-Ghent) can be seen beyond the verdant rolling hills of Lothersdale.

From the ridge a cairned path descends northwards

COWLING AND ICKORNSHAW

A farm lane descends from Lumb Head to Lower Summer House Farm (GR 966426 and not named on 1:50000 O.S. maps). A path across the fields then leads to the main Blackburn-Keighley road (A6068) and the small industrial town of Cowling, birthplace of Philip Snowden, first Labour Chancellor of the Exchequer.

Once off the main road, where the grim terraced houses are a little depressing, the place has real gritty Yorkshire character and is a mixture of rural and urban lifestyles, of farmyard and the mill. Cowling parish church lies peacefully by the beck, away from the scur-rying traffic on the main road.

Those who have the willpower to pass by the Black Bull public house, where reasonably priced bar snacks are provided, will cross the A6068, descend a field to Ickornshaw, pass the church and head northwards on the lane to Middleton.

COWLING HILL

The lane crosses Gill Beck with its lovely deciduous woodlands. It is abandoned here and a pleasurable path to the left traverses farmland to reach a country lane high on Cowling Hill. Looking back, the dark cliffs of Earls Crag and its twin monuments can clearly be seen,

Wainman's Pinnacle, a monument high on the hills above Cowling.

high on the valleysides with the dark Ickornshaw Moor rising behind.

The lane leads eastwards, taking the left fork at the first junction. After descending towards the valley of Surgill Beck it is left and a path (GR 962449) continues the descent more directly to cross the beautiful beck. It is a short climb to Woodhead Farm, where a track skirts the shoulder of an unnamed green hill.

LOTHERSDALE

Lothersdale is first spied from the brow of the hill although because it is so deeply set, its charms are not fully revealed until reaching the road at its centre. This quiet and pleasant village has much industrial heritage but its secluded position seems to have repelled the advances of the twentieth century. The picturesque stone terraced cottages are dominated by the tall mill chimney and tightly enclosed from the outside world

by emerald rolling hills. Lothersdale is a fine place to spend the night - a gentle place on this harsh journey.

The secluded village of Lothersdale.

Looking back on Stoodley Pike from the alternative route climbing up the hillsides from Lobb Mill, Todmorden.

THE CALDER VALLEY TO LOTHERSDALE
An Alternative Route via Boulsworth Hill

This is the 'high way' to reach Lothersdale and almost certainly the best. Black Hameldon and Boulsworth Hill are two fine moorland peaks and fitting places to say *au revoir* to the South Pennines.

CALDER VALLEY

The day begins on the eastbound towpath of the Rochdale Canal passing mills and factories on the route to Lobb Mill, where it is crossed. A path that zigzags on the steep slopes out of the busy Calder Valley commences at Lobb Mill Picnic Site (GR 956247), by the main road, close to the railway viaduct. The railway disappears through a tunnel at this point and its crossing becomes unnecessary. Height is rapidly gained on the firm track and the views beyond the crag and bracken-cloaked slopes to the Calder Valley improve. To the west the railway line, the Rochdale Canal and the busy road to Todmorden are all crowded by steep hill slopes. Stoodley Pike still dominates northern scenes, towering high above woodlands, stark mills and tall chimneys.

CROSS STONE

After passing some farm buildings the route follows an old walled track skirting a wooded ravine. The track is abandoned at GR 956251, where the ravine is circumvented by a path which can become muddy. This terminates at a country lane to the west of Cross Stone. An old church, which will probably have been noticed in views from Stoodley Pike, is passed. It is surprising and a little sad that, on close inspection, the building is found to be derelict - just a shell. Apparently the church, rebuilt in 1835, has been subjected to landslip and will probably be demolished.

A right turn is taken at a road junction before turning left on a track passing the golf course. What a wild place to play golf in the winter! The cragged pike of Whirlaw Stones crowns the skyline and the track continues in this direction, passing some old quarries. It meets the Calderdale Way amid sylvan scenes above the verdant hollow of Hole Bottom.

The route actually passes to the south of Whirlaw Stones on the open fells of Whirlaw Common but a

Descending from Black Hameldon with Pendle Hill on the horizon.

detour can be made to see them. Across the common, the track becomes paved with smooth slabs of millstone grit. This was an ancient pack-horse road and a few hundred years ago would have been used to convey coal from Cliviger and lime from Clitheroe. The track becomes enclosed again south of the Bride Stones, which are well worth a detour for they are some of the weirdest gritstone boulders north of the Dark Peak.

Shore Road is reached at GR 914274 by the 7th-century Celtic Mount Cross, which once marked a crossroads of ancient highways. Shore Road climbs northwards to reach the Long Causeway, a high lane linking Burnley with Hebden Bridge.

BLACK HAMELDON

At GR 913282, by a small stream, the route heads for Black Hameldon on a trackless course over rough grass and peaty terrain. The summit, Hoof Stones Height, lies at the southern end of the ridge. Except during dry periods, its concrete trig. point is surrounded by shallow pools. Unfortunately the broadness of the ridge restricts views of the nearby Calder Valley but there is

Looking back on the Gorple Upper Resrvoir and Black Hameldon.

has to be taken in avoiding the worst spots of its squelchy terrain. At the northern end the Cant Clough and Gorple Reservoirs come into view beneath dark hillslopes. The col between them is marked by millstone grit slabs, the Hare Stones (only named on 1:25000 maps). Beyond them is Hameldon, a grassy hill, interspersed with rashes of gritstone boulders and outcrops known as the Gorple Stones. Just discernible running beneath the stones is the Gorple Road, an ancient track from Worsthorne, which will guide us in a descent to the Widdop Reservoir.

compensation in the form of extensive panoramas including the peaks of Derbyshire, the Craven Hills (notably Pen-y-Ghent), and Lancashire's noble escarpment, Pendle Hill.

Progress northwards along Black Hameldon's broad ridge is quite easy-paced, although a modicum of care

HAMELDON
On the simple descent to Hare Stones, the wide views of East Lancashire's industrial conurbations, Burnley,

The Widdop Reservoir seen from the Gorple Road.

Weird boulders on the summit of Boulsworth Hill.

Padiham and Nelson, have captured centre-stage. At Hare Stones these views recede and are replaced by the rising spectacle of Hameldon and its interesting crags. One can easily imagine the travellers of bygone eras hurrying along this dark passage to the safe havens of Burnley or Hebden Bridge or perhaps the lonely Pack-Horse Inn (south-east of Widdop).

A marshy tract precedes the junction with the Gorple Road track, which then allows a very quick and easy pace eastwards, high above the Gorple Reservoirs.

WIDDOP RESERVOIR

The Widdop Reservoir lies in a huge, steep-sided bowl and is lined by dark gritstone crags. At GR 927325, above its southern shores, the path divides. Those wanting to rejoin the official Pennine Way can take the right hand track descending to the dam. From here it is a little less than a mile on the Hebden Bridge road to the intersection with the Pennine Way. The alternative route descends on a well defined path north-westwards to meet the road at GR 920337. The narrow road then straddles high moors before descending to GR 907353. Here a path is followed north-eastwards over rough grasslands to Will Moor, where it joins a wide, well-used track from the Coldwell Reservoirs. This traces the foot of Boulsworth Hill's northern slopes.

BOULSWORTH HILL

Being the highest hill in the area Boulsworth Hill's summit, known as Lad Law, is a worthwhile detour for it offers superb views over the plains and hills of Lancashire, Yorkshire and Derbyshire. If time is short continue along the track - both routes will meet at GR 927369.

For those who have opted to climb Boulsworth Hill, a Water Board concessionary path climbs from GR 922367 over the dull grassy slopes of Bedding Hill Moor to reach the boulder-laden top. After a short

The village of Wycoller makes a splendid detour from the alternative route at Boulsworth Hill. There is a café and B&B here and also a few interesting old bridges and buildings.

ridge walk eastwards to another group of boulders (the Little Chair Stones) a descent is made across Pot Brinks Moor before passing a small reservoir. Here a tarmac lane leads back to the track followed earlier (GR 927369) near to Spoutley Lumb Farm.

The track, in places paved with worn medieval millstone grit slabs, passes the remains of old lime kilns and through bare moorlands before turning northwards by Brinks End. Brinks End Farm enjoys a lofty position on the opposite banks of Turnhole Clough (only named on 1:25000 maps) and conjures up the spartan atmosphere typical of the Brontë novels.

After descending to ford the stream to the west of the farmhouse the track, muddy in places (after rain) continues between high pastures beneath Boulsworth's spartan northern flanks. It then veers south-eastwards into Smithy Clough (GR 949386 and not named on 1:50000).

THE WORTH VALLEY

From here the well waymarked Brontë Way is followed on a concessionary path, tracing the northern shores of the isolated Watersheddles Reservoir before following the valley bottom of the infant River Worth to Burnside Farm. The Brontë Way is now abandoned for a farm track, which climbs to the Stanbury road. A right turn here leads to the official route at Dean Fields to the north of the Ponden Reservoir. You could now aim for accommodation at Cowling or Lothersdale.

ROUTE FILE

Maps	OS.Landranger (1:50000) No 103 'Blackburn & Burnley'. Outdoor Leisure Map 21 'South Pennines' would again be useful.
Distance and time Official Route	18 miles (29km) 10 hours
Alternative via Black Hameldon	21 miles (35km) 11 hours
Terrain	Many ups and downs on steep cultivated hills north of Hebden Bridge before a return to peaty moors around Haworth. The alternative route visits two fine summits capping wild and woolly moors.
Accommodation	New Delight Inn at Jack Bridge (GR 963282); camping at Ponden Hall; B&Bs at Stanbury; B&Bs and camping at Cowling and Lothersdale; youth hostel off route at Earby; B&Bs at Cross Stone and Wycoller on the alternative route. Inns and B&Bs off route at Haworth.
Shops	At High Gate Farm, Blackshaw Head and Lothersdale. Also off route at Haworth.
Tourist Information	1 Bridge Gate, Hebden Bridge, West Yorkshire HX7 8EX. Tel. 0422 843831; or 2-4 West Lane, Haworth, West Yorkshire BD22 8EF. Tel 0535 42329

5

ACROSS ROLLING HILLS
Lothersdale to Malham

After trudging over the marshy gritstone moors of the Dark Peak and South Pennines, the verdant rolling countryside between Lothersdale and Malham is a pleasing contrast. There are no lofty mountains - Pinhaw Beacon at 1273ft (388m) is the highest - and the section is perhaps a break with the ideal of a High Pennine Traverse. It is, however, filled with little gems - the view from Pinhaw Beacon, where the outlines of famous Yorkshire Dales peaks urge one to lengthen the stride on easily graded footpaths; the lovely canal towpath walk at East Marton and the charming village of Gargrave on the banks of the River Aire, whose course is followed on that eagerly anticipated final approach to Malham and the high hills of Yorkshire.

Those who wish to continue the High Pennine theme can follow my alternative route, descending to the splendid market town of Skipton, 'Gateway to the Dales', before climbing to the heather-clad peaks of Embsay Moor. The craggy perch at Rylstone Fell offers fine views of the approach route to Malham across Hetton Common and the Weets. At the Weets we enter the fascinating limestone country of Craven.

The Canal at East Marton. One of the many picturesque and softer scenes on this section of the route.

LOTHERSDALE TO MALHAM
The Official Route

LOTHERSDALE

Leaving leafy Lothersdale behind we follow a path by the Hare and Hounds Inn heading northwards alongside a hedge and then a wall. It climbs across lush fields to meet a country lane south of Hewitts Farm.

PINHAW BEACON

After taking the approach lane to the farm, the path, guided by a dry-stone wall to the left, leads northwards to a stile at the edge of the open moors of Elsack to the east of Pinhaw Beacon. Locals often recall the yarn of Swine Harry when Pinhaw comes into conversation. This poor soul stole a pig and made his escape across the moor. In order to climb a stile he looped the pig's lead around his neck to leave both hands free. Unfortunately he stumbled at the top of the stile. Next morning he was found strangled by the weight of the beast who dangled from the opposite side.

Beyond a stile the route veers westwards to reach the summit of Pinhaw Beacon. The top, marked by a concrete trig. point and small cairn, is a grassy mound among extensive heather moors. The wide panoramas include Pendle and the hills of Bowland stretching out on the western horizon. In retrospective views southwards, the dark heather slopes of Ickornshaw Moor form a backdrop to the cliffs of Earl Crag. Northwards, beyond the plains of the Aire Valley, are the Craven Hills - those pale limestone peaks surrounding Malham on the southern edge of the Yorkshire Dales. Rising above them are the distinctive flat-topped peaks of Ingleborough and Pen-y-Ghent, instilling the desire to press on.

A well-defined track descends past an old quarry south-westwards to meet a cart track leading through more thick heather to the junction of two roads. The road to follow descends north-westwards until, at GR 934476, it is left for a Pennine Way signposted path descending Elsack's heather moors to Brown House Farm. The view ahead is pastoral, one of verdant hills, hedgerows, scattered cottages and farms.

THORNTON-IN-CRAVEN

Beyond Brown House Farm a lane leads to Thornton-in-Craven, an attractive village in pleasant surroundings. Unfortunately the village is in dire need of a by-pass for the busy A56 highway passes straight through the middle, destroying any semblance of serenity.

Leave Thornton along the Cam Road. This narrow metalled lane passes between picturesque cottages. After a couple of hundred yards it becomes a rutted

On the summit of Pinhaw Beacon looking north towards the peaks of the Yorkshire Dales.

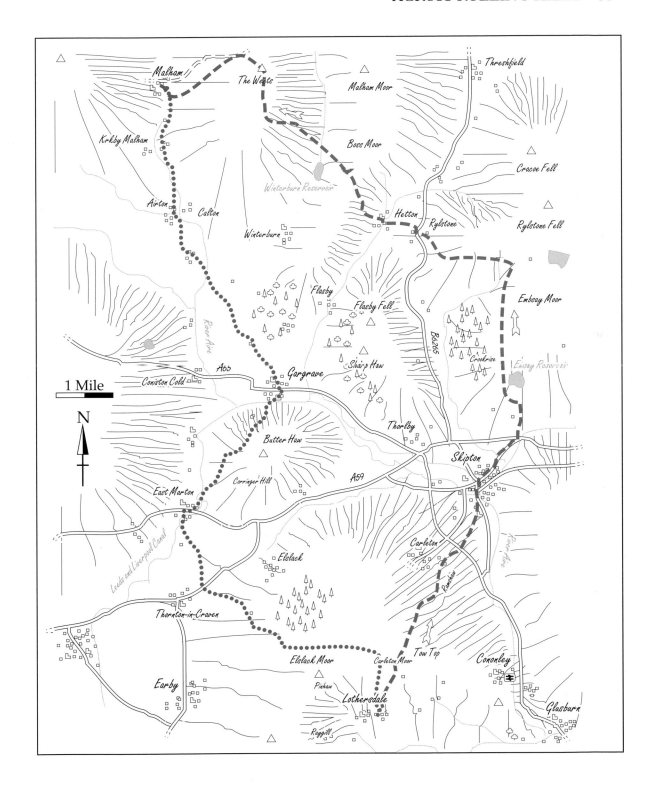

1 Mile

N

Malham
The Weets
Malham Moor
Threshfield
Kirkby Malham
Boss Moor
Cracoe Fell
Winterburn Reservoir
Airton
Calton
Winterburn
Hetton
Rylstone
Rylstone Fell
Flasby
Flasby Fell
Embsay Moor
River Aire
Gargrave
Sharp Haw
Crookrise
Embsay Reservoir
A65
Coniston Cold
B6265
Thorlby
Butter Haw
Skipton
A59
Corringer Hill
East Marton
Carleton
Leeds and Liverpool Canal
Elslack
Rumbтом
River Aire
Thornton-in-Craven
Elslack Moor
Carleton Moor
Tow Top
Cononley
Earby
Pinhaw
Lothersdale
Glusburn
Raygill

Above: Descending to the valley of Langber Beck.
Below: The canal near East Marton, whose parish church can be seen through the trees.

The River Aire at Gargrave - a delightful springtime scene.

track leading to rolling pastures. Beyond a stone-built barn, the track is left for a signposted path, which climbs lofty fields before descending to cross a small stream to the east of Langber Farm. We are now in the midst of lovely countryside that always reminds me of childhood picnics. It is very different from the high mountain environment synonymous with fellwalking but the change is somehow refreshing.

A stone slab bridge spans the stream and the succeeding footpath climbs on the western shoulder of Langber Hill (not named on 1:50000 maps) and thence down to the towpath of the Leeds-Liverpool Canal.

EAST MARTON

The official route uses the towpath only as far as the first bridge (No. 160). Here the bridge is crossed and a path followed through the church and village, crossing *en route* the busy A59 Liverpool to York road. The canal is met once more at bridge No. 162.

It is far more logical however to continue along the towpath thus omitting the unnecessary crossing of the

highway and the extra distance entailed. The canal is particularly beautiful along this stretch, embellished by brightly coloured boats. There is also a pleasantly sited café on the west side of bridge No. 162.

The towpath is abandoned beyond Williamson's Bridge and a stony lane followed for a couple of hundred yards. A cross-field path (signposted) then cuts the corner before rejoining the lane. The reacquaintance is short: just beyond a bridge adjacent to Trenet Laithe (a stone barn) the path climbs to high pastures whose undulations are accentuated by fences and small copses. The conical profiles of the Skipton Hills now form a very distinctive horizon.

GARGRAVE

At Scaleber Hill the views widen and the verdant Aire Valley stretches out below. The grey dwellings and church tower of Gargrave peep out from surrounding woodlands amid the valley pastures. A farm track east of Scaleber Farm is followed down the hillsides and thence over the Leeds-Kendal railway bridge. Beyond here a footpath crosses more fields westwards into

Malham Village.

Gargrave. These can be quite marshy after periods of heavy rainfall.

This splendid village by the banks of the River Aire is spoilt by the traffic of the A65 (Leeds-Kendal) road but there are proposals for a new by-pass. In contrast, the tree-lined river is quiet. It is especially beautiful in spring, decorated by daffodil blooms.

The lane northwards out of Gargrave passes over the Leeds-Liverpool Canal once more. It becomes a cart track north of Gargrave House and is abandoned beyond a small wood for a complex but well way-marked route across high rolling pastureland. It climbs

to Eshton Moor before descending to the Aire Valley, south of Newfield Hall.

From here the River Aire is crossed on a footbridge lying close to a country lane. Its western banks are traced to Newfield Bridge (GR 907582) where the route switches to the opposite side.

AIRTON

The centre of Airton is by-passed on the riverside route but there is a short uphill detour to see the Squatter's Cottage in the middle of the village green and also the Friends' Meeting House.

The Pennine Way meanwhile continues northwards, keeping to the Aire's eastern side and passing through the parkland of Hanlith Hall. Whether or not it is worth the half-mile detour from here to the village of Kirkby Malham will depend on the time of day and the condition of the walker. This secluded and unspoilt hamlet has an interesting fifteenth-century square-towered church, visited by Oliver Cromwell, whose name appears on its registers.

Prominent in views ahead are the gleaming ivory crags of the hillsides above Malham, our gateway to the spectacular limestone hills of the Yorkshire Dales.

MALHAM

On the final approach to Malham the route passes close to Aire Head Springs. The waters that gurgle

Rylstone Fell from the west.

On Hetton Common, looking back across the Winterburn Reservoir to the Flasby Fells.

from beneath the stones in a grassy hollow are the resurgence of the stream, which flows from the foot of Malham Cove and goes underground at Water Sinks.

Malham is a busy village - in the daytime tourists arrive in droves by coach and car. By early evening however, the crowds disappear, restoring peace and quiet to the place. At the centre of the village a single-arched, stone bridge spans Malham Beck. Cafés, inns, shops, a camp-site and youth hostel make this an ideal place to spend the night.

LOTHERSDALE TO MALHAM
An Alternative via Skipton Embsay Moor and Hetton Common

After an initial descent to Skipton in the Aire Valley this route returns to splendid hills at Embsay Moor. It must be noted however that Embsay Moor is part of the Chatsworth Estate and is an active grouse moor. Free access is allowed except on thirty days a year, when grouse shooting takes place. Nearly all these days fall between 12 August and the end of September, but never on a Sunday.

LOTHERSDALE
From the village inn turn east and downhill along the road passing the mill. At the bottom of the hill a gate to the left marks the start of a walled track that climbs to meet another rough track leading to the road close to Tow Top. After turning left along the road a right turn

is made along a track towards Tewitt Farm (marked Street Head on the map). Turn left before reaching the farmyard to a stile in the top left hand corner of the field. A dry stone wall then acts as a guide (the path changes sides twice) to a descent along the rough moorland spur of Ramshaw. Skipton looks splendid set in the verdant Aire Valley below, surrounded by shapely peaks. In late August splashes of purple heather add colour and contrast to the dark crags of Embsay Moor.

SKIPTON
Carleton Biggin Farm is passed to the left and its drive is used to reach the country lane by Butler Hill. This leads across the valley bottom to bustling Skipton.

EMBSAY
The best approach to Embsay is by the minor road past the caravan site and Yorkshire Dales Railway (worth seeing for its famous steam engines). Opposite the railway station entrance the main road through the village is left for a street which heads northwards. It terminates at a T-junction where you turn left, passing some enchanting cottages overlooking an old mill pond with attendant ever-ravenous ducks. The route continues on a stony track past the dam of the Embsay Moor Reservoir.

EMBSAY MOOR AND RYLSTONE FELL
A stile at the north-western end of the reservoir marks the start of the access land of Embsay Moor and signs list the restrictions. A narrow track through thick bracken climbs northwards up the steep flanks to reach

vast heather moors. After crossing the slight depression at the head of Waterfall Gill (not named on 1:50000 maps), the track climbs to some shelters on Brown Bank Brow, where it meets the bridleway traversing the moor between Rylstone and Bolton Abbey. Turn left here along the track through the heather to reach the gritstone edge of Rylstone Fell, just south of the wooden cross marking its summit (a good detour if you have time).

The path continues its descent to lower rough pastures. The right of way here leaves the track for a course (non-existent underfoot) south of a small pine plantation. Shortly after winding through a grassed-over quarry, it joins a farm road, which is followed northwards to Rylstone. The busy main road can be avoided by a well signposted (but slightly longer and muddier) cross-field path commencing at GR 974578. It emerges at a narrow lane close to the square-towered church.

HETTON
Country lanes lead from Rylstone to the sleepy village of Hetton. For lovers of good food, the Angel Inn is well worth a visit. A walled track known as Moor Lane (GR 963590) is followed north-westwards through flower-decked pastures. After about a mile and a half , the waters of Winterburn Reservoir appear to the left. The track terminates at a wall. Beyond is an intersection of five rights of way, though only four are visible underfoot. Our route, signposted to Malham, is a grassy path through reeds. It maintains the north-westerly direction, descending to a substantial stone bridge at the northern extremities of the Winterburn Reservoir. From here it climbs steadily over Hetton Common, parallel to Whetstone Gill. A few weather-beaten and gaunt-looking trees line the route to the right.

THE WEETS
The scrubby moorland on the final climb to the Weets is dull but short-lived. As the path veers right on the high western flanks of the hill to the summit trig. point, the views widen. The huge nick of Gordale Scar can now be seen across the rough moorland slopes to the north, while Malham nestles in a sheltered hollow beneath Kirkby Fell. We have arrived in North Yorkshire's limestone country.

A walled farm track is now used to descend to the country lane (Hawthorns Lane), which leads down to Gordale Scar. If you have decided not to come back this way tomorrow on the Kettlewell alternative, it is well worth a slight detour down the limestone ravine to see this magnificent craggy gorge and its waterfalls before descending to Malham.

NB Strong walkers on the alternative route wishing to make good time could also aim for Kilnsey or Kettlewell in Wharfedale. This could be done by scaling the cliffs by the waterfalls of Gordale Scar and following the well used footpath to Street Gate before turning eastwards down Mastiles Lane, a superb old green road which allows fast progress into Wharfedale via Kilnsey Crag.

MALHAM
Most walkers will prefer to visit the lovely village of Malham however. Although it is possible to use the road, a better way is to detour to view Janet's Fosse, a pretty twenty-foot waterfall set in a sylvan glen forged by Gordale Beck. From here a signposted riverside course leads through woods and fields down to the Pennine Way route at GR 902625. A well trodden path then leads northwards to Malham. Village

ROUTE FILE	
Maps	OS Landranger (1:50000) Nos 103 'Blackburn & Burnley' and 98 'Wensleydale'. OS Leisure Map No. 10 'Yorkshire Dales - Southern Area' would be helpful.
Distance and time Official Route Alternative via Skipton	15 miles (24km) 8 hours 18 miles (29km) 10 hours
Terrain	On the official route much of the day is spent in cultivated countryside. Field paths, canal towpaths and farm tracks are combined with a brief climb to the moors at Pinhaw Beacon. Beyond Skipton the alternative route is a stiffer mixture of high heather moorland and gritstone crag.
Accommodation	B&Bs and camping at Thornton-in-Craven, Gargrave and Malham. Youth hostel at Malham. On the alternative route there is a wide range of accommodation at Skipton and Malham.
Shops	Gargrave and Malham. On the alternative route at Skipton.
Tourist Information	8, Victoria Square, Skipton, North Yorkshire BD23 IJF. Tel. 0756 792809.

6

A WORLD OF LIMESTONE
Malham to Horton-in-Ribblesdale/Kettlewell

Leaving the beautiful village of Malham would be hard were it not for the magnetism of its magnificent cove and some lovely limestone hill-scapes on the route ahead.

The official Pennine Way heads northwards to the cove and the peaceful Malham Tarn before tackling the wild moors of Fountains Fell and the magnificently sculpted Pen-y-Ghent Hill. A descent is then made to the fine village of Horton-in-Ribblesdale which offers all the required creature comforts.

My alternative route is a more attractive proposition than the main route which, in the regions of Pen-y-Ghent, has become badly eroded. It explores more fully the dales for which Yorkshire is renowned and much cherished.

After visiting the awesome Gordale Scar the route threads through the limestone outcrops of Great Close and Out Pasture to the east of Malham Tarn. It then briefly descends to Arncliffe in Littondale before climbing to Old Cote Little Moor, which gives exquisite views of Wharfedale. Kettlewell, the next objective, lies dwarfed by high fells and limestone terraces in a landscape of green and ivory. It is, in my opinion, the prettiest large village in Yorkshire.

Pen-y-Ghent seen from near Horton Scar Lane. (Photo: Phil Iddon)

MALHAM TO HORTON-in-RIBBLESDALE
The Official Route

MALHAM and MALHAM COVE

Follow the narrow northbound lane out of Malham's village centre until, at GR 897633 you turn left for a signposted, recently renovated stony path which heads for Malham Cove across pastureland. The cove is a spectacular amphitheatre - a natural construction in ivory crag. Malham Beck trickles from the foot of the cliffs and placidly flows through the verdant meadows to the right of the footpath. An 'improved' path climbs steeply in a series of steps to the top of the cove where there is an expansive area of limestone pavements. The grikes or channels in the pavements are often filled with plant life, including hart's tongue ferns. The massive scale of the cove is evident from the top and most walkers linger here - some to watch the climbers clawing their way up the vertical ramparts. Views to the south and west include Pendle Hill, Bowland and the crazed field patterns of the Ribble and Aire Valleys.

Since Wainwright's advice in his *Pennine Way Companion*, most travellers have chosen to ignore the official Pennine Way from the top of the Cove and instead head north-westwards along the dry valley. I agree that this route is scenically preferable but for the purists who want to follow in Tom Stephenson's footsteps, the other route continues past the eastern end of the cove and takes a parallel course over Malham Lings. Both routes are well signposted to Malham Tarn.

The dry valley is an interesting ice-sculpted channel lined with curious crags and bluffs. At its head the path zig-zags below Combe Hill (not marked on 1:50000 maps) and then follows a dry-stone wall to Water Sinks, where the gurgling stream from Malham Tarn goes underground.

MALHAM TARN

Beyond Water Sinks a narrow lane is encountered.

Malham Cove, a gigantic amphitheatre of limestone and perhaps the most spectacular sight on the whole walk.

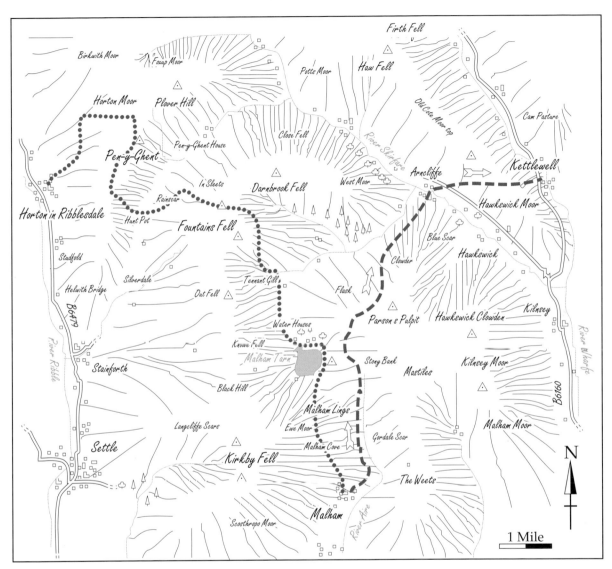

After going right along it and crossing the stream the Pennine Way is rejoined at GR 897658. The path then goes northwards across a grassy plain to meet a wide stony track, which is followed to the eastern banks of Malham Tarn. The expansive lake, flanked by woods, wetlands and craggy limestone cliffs, is a haven for wild life and the area is now a bird sanctuary and nature reserve.

After entering delightful mixed woodland, the track passes behind Malham Tarn House, a favourite haunt of the writer Charles Kingsley, author of *The Water*

Babies. The huge Victorian mansion is owned by the National Trust and also used as a field study centre.

FOUNTAINS FELL

Leaving the woodland, the path crosses fields northwards to reach the Stainforth to Arncliffe lane, situated on a high wild pass at the head of the valley of Cowside Beck. Ahead is Fountains Fell, so named because it was once owned by Fountains Abbey. From here the fell is featureless, its drab green slopes relieved only by sparse limestone crags. To the east of the crags, and set back a

On the north slopes of Fountains Fell with Pen-y-Ghent behind.

Pen-y-Ghent from above Dale Head.

couple of hundred yards from the lane, is the secluded Tennant Gill Farm.

The farm is circumvented and the succeeding path meanders up the grassy eastern flanks of Fountains Fell, passing to the north of its true summit. The heather-clad, peaty plateau is quite expansive and very desolate in the regions of its tarn, which lies in a slight depression. On reaching the firm northern regions of the fell several tall stone cairns are encountered. The surrounding area was once mined for coal - the deep shafts remain but are fenced off in the interests of safety.

The most spectacular feature of Fountains Fell is its view of Pen-y-Ghent (Welsh for Hill of the Winds). This long escarpment soars above the barren plains of Silverdale in steep grassy slopes broken by scree and two distinct lines of crag forming two steps on the western edge of its profile. Behind lies Ingleborough, a flat-topped peak, looking inferior in comparison. Great Whernside and Buckden Pike sprawl across the eastern horizon beyond a series of wide peaty ridges

and the depression that is Wharfedale. No time to dwell: we must press on!

A good stony path descends westwards passing an uncharacteristically rocky area before meeting the Stainforth to Halton Gill lane at GR 853723. A mile of road walking follows - fast and easy. Then the road is abandoned for a track which passes close to Dale Head Farm, whose dramatic setting beneath Pen-y-Ghent has inspired many photographers and artists.

PEN-Y-GHENT HILL

Beyond Dale Head, the path is of an easy gradient all the way to the ridge south of Pen-y-Ghent's summit massif. From here the fell appears as a craggy colossus, its twin steps rising boldly to the skies. The 'Way' now climbs steeply among the crags which are pale limestone in the lower regions and darker gritstone closer to the summit. A dry-stone wall leads from the edge of the grassy plateau to the summit itself. Ingleborough and Whernside, the other two of those infamous 'Three Peaks', capture one's attention, standing out

(Photo: Phil Iddon)

The Horton Scar Road Pen-y-Ghent. (Photo: Phil Iddon)

among more featureless moors and escarpments, which decline to the plains of West Yorkshire and the Ribble Valley.

The descent to Horton-in-Ribblesdale is studded with superb features. It initially heads north-westwards to the escarpment's edge and continues above precipitous gritstone cliffs.

HUNT AND HULL POTS
At a break in the cliffs, the path descends westwards to traverse rolling moorland. A few yards off route, at the northern end of the moorland, is Hunt Pot, easily recognized by the surrounding wire fence. The dark aperture is 15ft long by 6ft wide and swallows a stream which then plumbs its 200 ft depths.

Beyond Hunt Pot the path continues north-westwards, passing through a gate in a dry-stone wall encountered near an isolated shooting hut. Another worthwhile detour to the north-east leads to Hull Pot, an open chasm measuring 300ft by 60ft with a 60ft depth. After rainy periods the stream, which is other-

wise subterranean, adds drama to the scene in the form of an impressive waterfall

Retrace your steps to the shooting hut and follow the Horton Scar Lane, a pleasant walled track, to Horton-in-Ribblesdale. In this popular village are many

Above the cloud on the summit of Pen-y-Ghent.

Above: Janet's Fosse, near Malham.
Below: By the waterfalls in Gordale Scar. (Photo: Phil Iddon)

Yew Cougar Scar with Arncliffe peering through the haze.
(Photo: Phil Iddon)

amenities including a youth hostel, two inns, a café, and a shop.

MALHAM TO KETTLEWELL
An Alternative Route via Arncliffe

The route via Pen-y-Ghent is one of the finest sections on the official Pennine Way but this alternative is scenically superior. There are no badly eroded paths such as those around Pen-y-Ghent. From lofty limestone hilltops you will see the very best of Yorkshire's verdant dales.

MALHAM

Everybody who visits Malham will want to view the magnificent cove (for directions see the previous section). From the top of the cove, continue along the limestone pavements and thence on a well defined path south-eastwards to meet a country lane (GR 903637). On the opposite side of the lane the path continues beneath rocky outcrops to reach Gordale Bridge just west of Gordale Scar.

GORDALE SCAR

If you haven't seen it already, it is worth making a detour across the road to see Janet's Fosse, a lovely little waterfall set in a shady bower. The route continues northwards from the Gordale Bridge along a stony track to Gordale Scar, passing a camp-site before entering a hollow, surrounded by high grassy slopes and towering limestone cliffs. Alongside, a shallow stream gurgles over its rocky bed, with patchy wetlands of watercress nearby. Turn the corner and suddenly the true magnificence of the gorge is revealed. The pale precipices have closed in dramatically to form a dark defile. Gordale Beck twists and turns among the confines of the narrow chasm, cascading over crags and boulder beds. On lofty but narrow grassy ledges, yew trees cling precariously to the cliffs. At the waterfall, a short but easy scramble is necessary to reach the upper scree-strewn path, which climbs steeply out of the cauldron and into the light.

The well-defined path continues along the western edge of Gordale Beck's interesting rocky ravine before veering north-westwards on a wide grassy path to Street Gate, a crossroads of cart tracks.

GREAT CLOSE AND OUT PASTURE
The northbound track traversing the high pastures of Great Close is followed to the east of Great Close Scar.

It is abandoned at GR 907675, close to Middle House Farm, which lies beneath the lower crags of Parson's Pulpit. A path then continues northwards to a lonely, derelict cottage, north of which there is a meeting of routes. We take the bridleway on the right which climbs north-north-eastwards to the rough moorland environs of Out Pasture, where it descends to a hollow and threads through the limestone bluffs of Flask and Dew Bottoms. Below, in the northern landscape, Cowside Beck flows in a deep valley dominated by the green masses of Darnbrook Fell and Fountains Fell. A high metalled lane, linking Arncliffe and Stainforth, skirts the hillsides high above the beck.

ARNCLIFFE
The path, which is here known as the Monk's Road, gradually descends the slopes of Clowder at the edge of Yew Cougar Scar. Soon a village appears in a wide green vale beneath rocky terraces and partially wooded slopes. This is Arncliffe and the pleasant valley is Littondale.

Beyond Yew Cougar Scar the path drops steeply to the flat fields south of the village. A farm track then

Arncliffe Church and the River Skirfare.

Kettlewell seen from the crags of Middlesmoor Pasture.

leads to the village green, passing the Falcon Inn, once the Woolpack Inn of Emmerdale Farm fame.

The beautiful tree-lined River Skirfare is crossed on the old stone road bridge and a path then traces its far banks to reach the Halton Gill lane. Arncliffe's stone square-towered parish church can be seen through the trees.

OLD COTE LITTLE MOOR

A narrow path on the opposite side of the lane rakes across fields on a climb that continues in the shelter of Byre Bank Wood. On leaving the wood it climbs among the limestone crags to attain the rough open fells of Old Cote Little Moor. The secrets of Wharfedale are slowly revealed after passing the crest of this spur. The two high fells on the other side of the valley are Buckden Pike and Great Whernside, whose craggy flanks are cut by Dowber Gill (not named on 1:50000 maps) and Park Gill.

KETTLEWELL

A descent is made across Middlesmoor Pasture to the edge of limestone terraces overlooking the valley. Here is a place to pause and admire the aerial view of Kettlewell, an enchanting village close to the River Wharfe, which meanders lazily among green fields. Broad-leaved trees and dry-stone walls hug the graceful sweeping hillslopes. The path enters a mini-defile in the limestone terrace before raking across grassy slopes to the river's edge close to the road bridge on the western side of the village. Many will want to stay the night at one of the fine inns or camp-site - most will want to explore Kettlewell's narrow streets and charming shops.

ROUTE FILE	
Maps	OS Landranger (1:50000) No. 98 'Wensleydale'. OS Leisure Map No. 10 'Yorkshire Dales - Southern Area' would be helpful although the last section between Pen-y-Ghent's summit and Horton is interupted.
Distance and time Official Route Alternative Route	14 miles (23km) 9 hours 10 miles (16km) 6 hours
Terrain	Easy walking on firm limestone hill and dale paths but a stiff climb on the upper slopes of Pen-y-Ghent.
Accommodation	B&Bs, couple of inns, a camp-site and youth hostel at Horton; B&Bs and an inn at Arncliffe and B&Bs, a few of inns, a campsite and youth hostel at Kettlewell.
Shops	Horton and Kettlewell. On the alternative route at Skipton.
Tourist Information	8, Victoria Square, Skipton, North Yorkshire BD23 IJF. Tel. 0756 792809.

7

STRIDING OUT TO WENSLEYDALE

Horton-in-Ribblesdale/Kettlewell to Hawes

Both official and alternative routes continue over the magnificent limestone peaks of the Yorkshire Dales in what many regard as the finest Pennine scenery. The official Pennine Way climbs out of Ribblesdale on a green road, passing fascinating caves and pot-holes. It continues over lonely moors on the old Roman 'Cam High Road' rising to Dodd Fell. The finale is an easy-paced descent to Hawes, a busy little market-town set in the beautiful wide valley of Wensleydale.

For those who want to be on the high tops, I have included an alternative itinerary which includes Buckden Pike, which at 2302 ft (702m), is the highest peak to be tackled so far.

In foul weather there is a valley alternative along the banks of the River Wharfe. Both meet at the little hamlet of Cray, where an ancient track straddles Stake Moss before descending to Yorkshire's largest natural lake, Semer Water, situated in tranquil Raydale. A steep climb to Wether Fell and its Roman road is rewarded with truly spectacular panoramas of Wensleydale, views which persist throughout the delightful final approaches to Hawes.

Walkers following official Pennine Way on the West Cam Road over Dodd Fell. (Photo: Phil Iddon)

On the West Cam Road, Dodd Fell with the hills of Wensleydale in the distance.

HORTON-IN-RIBBLESDALE TO HAWES
The Official Route

HORTON-IN-RIBBLESDALE

The route now utilizes the Horber Scar Lane, a walled track, which begins at the Crown Hotel and climbs northwards on the eastern slopes of Ribblesdale. Pen-y-Ghent's precipitous western facade towers boldly above the grassy expanses of Horton Moor to the right. In the opposite direction the more spacious views across Ribblesdale are dominated by Ingleborough,

Jackdaw Hole.

whose flat-topped summit plateau just rises above Simon Fell's flanks (the view is once again marred by those awful quarries!).

After a mile the track passes the Sell Gill Holes, where Sell Gill Beck plunges into a deep chasm to the east of the track. Immediately to the west is its other entrance.

Jackdaw Hole, three quarters of a mile further north, has a larger aperture and its vertical limestone walls are surrounded by trees. When last there, I was lucky enough to be able to study a pair of young kestrels who were obviously in residence.

On Birkwith Moor, at GR 813772, a Pennine Way signpost by a gate points westwards across open moor. A forestry track continues to Old Ing Farm, where an old drovers' road leads northwards once more.

Steps in a stone wall allow the viewing of Calf Holes (sometimes known as Dry Laithe Cave). Here a stream flowing over a rocky bed cascades down the deep and dark pot to a pool at its base. The subterranean passage then emerges at Browgill Cave to the north-east.

LING GILL

A mile to the north along the old road is Ling Gill, where a boisterous stream flows at the bottom of a heavily wooded ravine. It is a nature reserve and within its fenced-off confines a multitude of wild flowers grow. To the north, the path crosses over an old stone

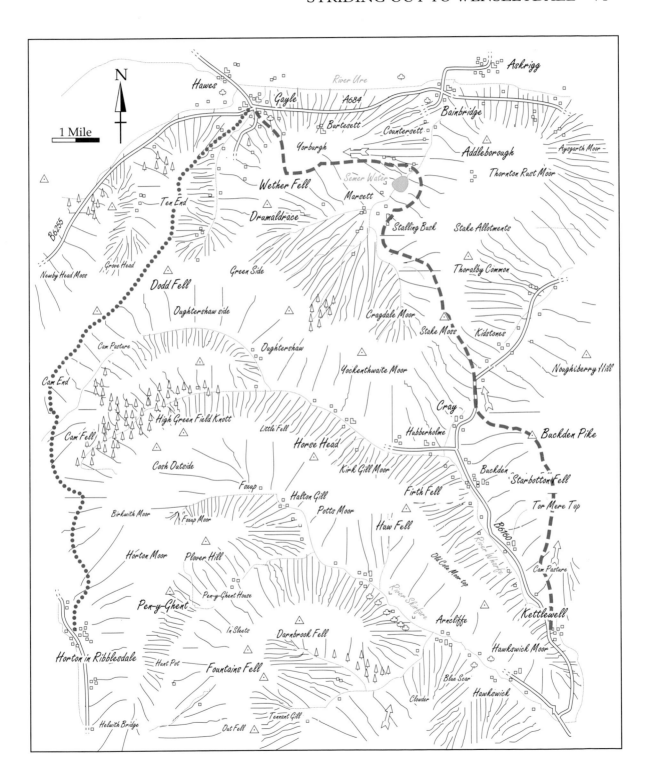

Hawes in the early morning sunshine.

pack-horse bridge. This area makes an outstanding natural camp-site as Wainwright pointed out in his Pennine Way guide. The accumulation of camping garbage is testament that his words were heeded.

CAM FELL

Beyond Ling Gill Bridge the track climbs the grassy inclines to meet the Cam High Road (Roman road) at Cam End. To the west is the huge Ribblehead Viaduct, which conveys the famous Settle to Carlisle railway. Beyond it lies the whaleback ridge of Whernside and to the south is the unmistakable profile of Ingleborough. The view westwards is less pleasant, containing ill-planned spruce forests enshrouding the wild moorland habitat of Langstrothdale. For the next mile the Pennine Way shares the same path as the newer Dales Way. (The latter then diverts, descending towards Cam Houses by the conifer plantations in the valley of Outershaw - the remote farm offers accommodation and refreshments).

DODD FELL

Beyond the farm's access road the Cam Road is met-alled and conveys motor traffic to and from Hawes in Wensleydale. At GR 829834 our route leaves it to fol-low the West Cam Road, skirting the west side of Dodd Fell above the fascinating valley of Snaizeholme Beck. Here small, sympathetically designed spruce forests add a little splash of colour and emphasize the form of the hillsides.

GAYLE

At Ten End, the northern edge of Dodd Fell, the track is left and a cairned path on grassy hill slopes descends north-eastwards, giving absolutely superb views of ver-dant Wensleydale. The villages of Gayle and Hawes seem diminutive in comparison with the massive flanks of Great Shunner Fell and the limestone cliffs of Pike Hill. The large Gaudy House Farm is passed and a track (Gaudy Lane) continues east then north to meet a lane at GR 865892. This can be followed to Gayle, or alternatively the official and fussy line can be traced across fields from Gaudy Lane at GR 865889, passing by the village centre.

HAWES

At GR 870895, a signposted path leaves the road link-ing Gayle and Hawes, crossing a field and passing close to St Margaret's Church before emerging on Hawes' main street. The bustling market-town has a wide choice of shops, cafés and inns. It would be wise to stock up here because the next sizeable place on the route is Middleton-in-Teesdale, some 34 miles (54km) distant.

KETTLEWELL TO HAWES
An Alternative Route

A fine mountain route for those trying to reach Hawes in one day climbs northwards out of the village on the old walled track to Buckden Pike, one of Yorkshire's finest viewpoints.

KETTLEWELL
The Coverdale Road, signposted to Leyburn is followed to a sharp bend (GR 972725). From here we switch to a walled stony track known as the Top Mere Road, which climbs steadily over a high grassy spur separating the valleys of Wharfedale and Park Gill. Looking back, Kettlewell sits snugly, surrounded by walled pastures gently contouring the tree-studded hill slopes. The valley is enclosed by the terraced limestone crags of Old Cote Moor to the west and the majestic, soaring slopes of Great Whernside to the east.

CAM HEAD
At Cam Head the track meets the Starbotton Road and a left turn is made. Just beyond a gate (GR 965753) the old road is abandoned for a track that climbs north-north-eastwards and then northwards across Starbotton Out Moor, high above the huge hollow formed by Cam Hill Beck. Eastern views are obscured by Tor Mere Top but to the west Wharfedale is laid beneath your feet..

After passing the spoil heaps of old lead mines, the path joins the old Walden Road at the head of Cam Gill (GR 962772) and the route follows this north-eastwards over Starbotton Fell. On attaining the ridge there are attractive views down the Walden Valley, one of the few in these parts to be unaffected by tourism and the twentieth century.

Beyond a gate at GR 965776 the Walden Road is abandoned for a path that climbs north-westwards over brown peaty moorland towards the summit plateau of Buckden Pike.

THE MEMORIAL CROSS
Sited on the southern end of Buckden Pike's summit massif is a solitary cross and plaque - a memorial to the Polish crew of a Second World War aeroplane which crashed into the fell during a violent snow storm. There was one survivor. He had sustained a broken leg, but crawled out of the wreckage and found some fox's tracks. On deducing that in such harsh weather the fox

Kettlewell seen from the low slopes of Great Whernside.

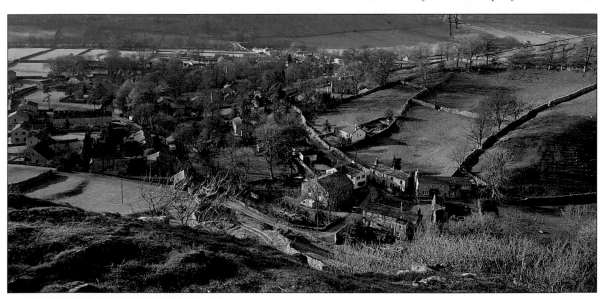

Above: On the summit of Buckden Pike with Fountains Fell, Pen-y-Ghent and Ingleborough on the horizon.
Below: The hamlet of Cray seen on the descent of Buckden Pike.

would be looking for easy pickings close to human civilization, he followed the footprints, which did indeed lead to a farmhouse. In thanksgiving for his own life and in memory of his five colleagues, he had the cross erected on the site of the crash.

Semer Water and Addleborough seen from the slopes of Wether Fell.

BUCKDEN PIKE

After passing the Memorial Cross, the wall is followed to Buckden Pike's summit. The summit is crowned by a cairn and trig. point. From it there are superb views westwards down the spine of Pen-y-Ghent to Ingleborough, while to the north is the great whaleback of Whernside and the craggy Wild Boar Fell.

It is decision time again - whether to use the East Dales Loop route down into Waldendale and onwards to Avsgarth and Reeth (*see* Appendix) or to head for Hawes, where the official route is rejoined. The Hawes route is rougher and higher but the loop is scenically superior.

Unless you have decided to follow the East Dales Loop the initial descent on the Hawes route from Buckden Pike is guided by a dry-stone wall down the steep western flanks. Signposts and a line of wooden stakes make the well used path easy to follow as it changes direction, gradually veering to the south-west.

On further descent, the village of Cray appears, tucked close in to the sides of Cow Pasture. Walls radiate from the village fields to the high moors rather like a section from a huge spider's web. In the valley below, Cray Gill tumbles in a series of picturesque waterfalls to meet the River Wharfe, which meanders in low plains beneath wooded lower hill slopes of Yockenthwaite Moor.

CRAY

The mountain path meets a well-used ancient road known as Buckden Rake at GR 941785. Here we double-back north-eastwards along the rake passing some waterfalls *en route* to Cray Bridge (GR 944797). A short signposted detour can be made to Cray village and the pleasant White Lion Inn for those who are in need of sustenance - otherwise we continue to the road.

STAKE MOSS

At GR 943804, on the high pass between Wharfedale and Bishopdale, the road is abandoned for an ancient walled track, known as Gilbert Lane. The track is a firm one and a good pace can be achieved climbing to Stake Moss, whose summit plateau is sparsely set with limestone clints. A footpath seems to cut the corner across Cragdale Allotments but it is better to stick to the track, which gives superior views and is quicker. Glimpses of Raydale and the tiny village of Marsett are seen as the track descends high above the valley of Cragdale Water.

STALLING BUSK and SEMER WATER

Semer Water, one of Yorkshire's few large lakes, appears as the track curves northwards. This little jewel set in the quiet valley of Raydale is Yorkshire's largest natural lake. The village of Stalling Busk can be seen languishing high above the southern shores while at the far end, beneath the crags of Common Allotments, is Countersett.

On meeting the lane at Stalling Busk two options are available and both meet at the Cam High Road at GR 886874. It is possible to go on a more direct route to Marsett and climb steeply up the slopes of Common Allotments, or alternatively take a more leisurely route passing by the northern shores of Semer Water. I prefer the latter.

On this route, a left turn is made through the village centre and thence northwards on a path descending to the old chapel ruins on the valley floor. The chapel was built in 1722 on the site of an older church but was abandoned for a new more central church in 1902.

The path continues through the meadows of Raydale and alongside the banks of Semer Water to

On the old Roman road on Wether Fell.   *Gale with Wether Fell behind.*

meet the lane once more at Low Blean. The lane, which climbs steeply past Countersett, is followed to GR 913878, where it bends towards the spur of Bainbridge High Pasture. The footpath then leads eastwards climbing to the foot of some unnamed crags. The views across Raydale and Semer Water are at their most exquisite from here and include the imposing, flat-topped limestone escarpment of Addleborough, whose lower slopes partially obscure the valley of Wensleydale.

WETHER FELL

The path now traverses the high moors of Common Allotments and emerges on the Roman Cam High Road. This once carried Roman legions from forts at Chester to Carlisle. After crossing the ancient road, the route continues across Wether Fell. A rutted track is met and followed to the western side of the craggy knoll of Yorburgh where impressive panoramas of Wensleydale are revealed. Great Shunner Fell and Lovely Seat are seen sprawling from the village of Hawes to dominate the skyline.

GAYLE AND HAWES

By Yorburgh the track is left for a footpath which descends north-westwards across high meadows. A gap-stile in the dry-stone wall to the left marks the spot. The route underfoot is obscure in places but, if a bee-line is made directly towards Gayle, a well-defined grassy path from GR 875887 will then lead down to a narrow walled track at the corner of some woods. This, in turn, descends through colourful flower-covered

meadows to Gayle where the official route is met.

NB In bad weather the best option from Kettlewell would be to follow valley paths to the east of the road to Starbotton and west of the river from there to Buckden. A path then climbs past Rakes Wood to the Bishopdale Road at GR 944797.

Also note that an East Dales Traverse begins from the alternative route on Buckden Pike visiting Aysgarth and Reeth before meeting with the official routes east of Tan Hill (time about 3 days from Kettlewell). *See* Appendix.

ROUTE FILE	
Maps	OS.Landranger (1:50000) No 98 'Wensleydale'. OS Leisure Map No.30 'Yorkshire Dales - Northern & Central Areas' would be helpful on this and the next section to Tan Hill.
Distance and time Official Route	14 miles (22km) 8 hours
Alternative via Buckden Pike	17 miles (28km) 10 hours
Terrain	The official route is fairly easy. Its climbs are gradual and mainly on well-graded tracks. More climbing is involved in the alternative which tackles Buckden Pike fairly directly.
Accommodation	B&Bs, inns, camp-sites and a youth hostel at Hawes. Inn at Cray in addition on the alternative route.
Shops	Hawes.
Tourist Information	8, Victoria Square, Skipton, North Yorkshire BD23 1JF . Tel. 0756 792809

8

HIGH FELLS AND WATERFALLS

Hawes to Tan Hill

This section crosses the bleaker northern reaches of the Yorkshire Dales to the border of County Durham at Tan Hill, the highest pub in England.

The official way visits the impressive waterfall of Hardraw Force before scaling the expansive peat mosses of Great Shunner Fell - a little bit of Derbyshire in the Dales and a place that will be remembered for its superb panoramas across the fells of Yorkshire, Durham and Cumbria. From this lofty perch we descend to the sleepy hamlet of Thwaite in Upper Swaledale. Kisdon Hill, a lovely little limestone peak, is then circumvented on a course high above the river leading to the most exciting section on the approach to Keld. Here the waters of the Swale begin to race and tumble in a series of waterfalls, beautifully situated in a narrow wooded glen.

From Keld the official Pennine Way steers clear of the main watershed, choosing instead to skirt around the shoulders of Stonesdale Moor to Tan Hill.

On the alternative route, Great Shunner Fell has been omitted for the craggy Pike Hill and the Butter Tubs Pass. After descending to the village of Muker, the route continues on the east banks of the Swale before entering the gorge of Swinner Gill. Here an old miners' track continues to Gunnerside Gill and climbs to the remote tops of Punchard Head and West Moor.

The mines at Swinner Gill on the alternative route east of Keld.

HAWES TO TAN HILL
The Official Route via Great Shunner Fell

HAWES

Hawes is a busy market town. If supplies are required, get them here for it is 34 miles (54km) to the next sizeable place, Middleton-in-Teesdale. The prospect before us is a short level walk across lanes and fields to Hardraw, which lies snugly beneath Wensleydale's northern slopes.

After taking the Hardraw road out of the village to a point just north of the disused railway, the official Pennine Way follows a path across fields to the left. In fact this just cuts a corner and rejoins the road a little short of Haylands Bridge. The twin-arched stone bridge spanning the River Ure is crossed and a Pennine Way signpost once again directs us to cross more lowland pasture towards Hardraw.

HARDRAW

At the back of Hardraw's little inn, the Green Dragon, is England's highest waterfall, Hardraw Force. It is a spectacle not to be missed, but to see it you will have to pass through the inn and pay a nominal toll.

Unexpectedly, prior to reaching the waterfall, there is a circular stone bandstand. This is the setting for the popular annual Hardraw Force Brass Band Competition with entries from bands all over Yorkshire and the neighbouring counties.

The Force is really impressive, especially after heavy rains. It cascades 96ft in one step over tree-fringed limestone crags to a dark pool below. For those who want a different perspective, it is possible to walk along a shelf to a sheltered alcove behind the falls without getting wet. In 1890, after disastrous floods the lip of Hardraw Force was destroyed allowing the river to alter its course and rush down to the base in a series of cascades. The landowner, Lord Wharncliffe, restored the situation by instigating the reconstruction of the lip to restore the spectacle to its former glory.

GREAT SHUNNER FELL

Beyond Hardraw, a track bound by dry-stone walls is followed on the long trek up the massive moorland expanses of Great Shunner Fell. Initially the route is interesting with good retrospective views of Hawes and Wensleydale. Later Ingleborough peeps over the shoulder of Widdale Fell.

When the open fellsides are reached the walk loses its appeal. It is a long way to the summit and little changes, for Great Shunner's concave slopes conceal the summit mass until the very end. In many places the grassy slopes are badly eroded and the brown gooey peat breaks through to the surface - reminiscent of the conditions on the Dark Peak plateaux of Derbyshire.

Reaching the summit lifts the gloom. Great Shunner

On the summit of Great Shunner Fell with Ingleborough on the horizon.

is the highest hill so far encountered on the Pennine Way - 2340 ft (713m) - and its elevation affords superb panoramas in all directions. The Northern Pennines from Mickle Fell to Cross Fell are revealed behind the dusky moorland spread of Nine Standards Rigg. In southern vistas the Three Peaks of Yorkshire, Pen-y-Ghent, Ingleborough and Whernside all figure on the horizon, rising above lower and less distinctive fells. Looking over the neighbouring Hugh Seat to the west are the jagged fells of Lakeland. To the east is

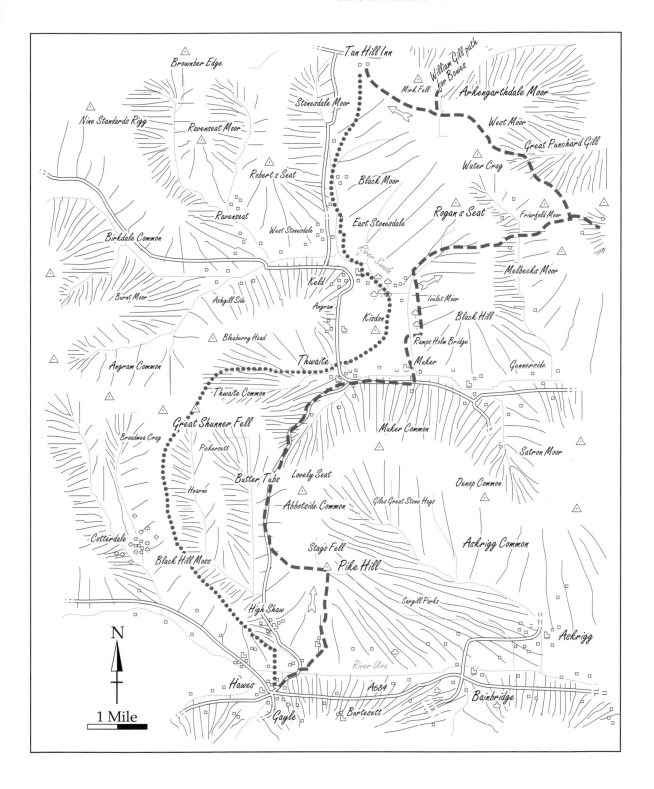

Brownber Edge

Tan Hill Inn

William Gill path for Bowes

Mirk Fell

Arkengarthdale Moor

Stonesdale Moor

Nine Standards Rigg

Ravenseat Moor

West Moor

Robert's Seat

Black Moor

Water Crag

Great Punchard Gill

Ravenseat

West Stonesdale

East Stonesdale

Rogan's Seat

Friarfold Moor

Birkdale Common

River Swale

Melbecks Moor

Keld

Burnt Moor

Ashgill Side

Angram

Ivelet Moor

Kisdon

Black Hill

Bleaberry Head

Ramps Holm Bridge

Muker

Gunnerside

Angram Common

Thwaite

Thwaite Common

Great Shunner Fell

Muker Common

Satron Moor

Broadmea Crag

Pickersett

Oxnop Common

Butter Tubs

Lovely Seat

Hearne

Giles Great Stone Hags

Askrigg Common

Abbotside Common

Cotterdale

Stags Fell

Black Hill Moss

Pike Hill

Sargill Parks

Askrigg

High Shaw

River Ure

N

Hawes

A684

Bainbridge

1 Mile

Gayle

Burtesett

Above: Leaving Thwaite in Swaledale for Kisdon Hill.
Left: East Gill Force, one of the many splendid waterfalls around the village of Keld.

lovely Swaledale and that is our next objective - things are looking up!

The descent from the summit is also lengthy but, being downhill, a good pace can be made. The path declines north-eastwards on peat-hagged, grassy moors with Thwaite Beck cutting deep into the fellsides to the right. Gradually the course veers eastwards with the prospect of Swaledale opening up in views ahead.

THWAITE

Above Moor Close, a walled cart track is joined which takes us down to the road just north of Thwaite. A right turn along the lane leads to the charming village where a huddled group of old stone cottages cling to the sheltered hillsides in this quiet corner of the dale.

For those who want to tarry, there is B&B accommodation here. A further mile-and-a-half away, at Muker, is a camp-site and inn.

KISDON HILL

From Thwaite's village centre, adjacent to the small church, the route continues eastwards past a couple of cottages before entering fields and striking north-eastwards towards the slopes of Kisdon Hill. A Pennine

Looking south-east along Swaledale from Kisdon Hill between Thwaite and Keld.

Way sign at the foot of the hill indicates a narrow path raking through slopes of bracken and heather before reaching the high farm of Kisdon. Here retrospective views show Thwaite's sheltered position tucked in a cosy fold at the foot of Great Shunner Fell. Almost all the fields in sight have their small stone-built barn for wintering stock. It is, I am told, a feature of Swaledale.

To the east of Kisdon Farm is Kisdon Cottage. From here a sign points the way northwards, high on the hillside above the River Swale, which has changed course to thread through a tight valley bound on its eastern side by Black Hill. The prospects from here are superb. Beyond the village of Muker, Swaledale is spread before you, paling to the plains of Richmond while, to the north, the partially wooded valley leads the eye to the outcrops and bluffs of Swinner Gill.

The path northwards is one of the highlights of the Dales' traverse so far and picks its way on a high shelf though bracken and rashes of limestone boulders. It then declines north-westwards towards Keld and the rushing River Swale. Swinner Gill's disused old lead-mine workings can be seen to good advantage as can

the ruins of Crackpot Hall, perched precariously on high hill slopes opposite.

KELD

Keld first appears furtively tucked behind woodlands, which envelop the Swale hereabouts. The sound of its famous waterfalls filters through the trees. For those who want to see Kisdon Force, the most impressive of Keld's numerous waterfalls, a path doubles back to the riverbank, but you have to retrace your steps. An old lane, which can be muddy at times, leads to the village centre. Those who do not wish to see the village can turn right at a signposted path, descending to cross the Swale via a little footbridge.

Those who visit Keld will have to return to this path. Hereabouts the lively river is confined by limestone cliffs and thick woodland. Close by is the impressive East Gill Force, which tumbles from the hillsides to join the Swale.

From the bridge the path continues to the east of the fine waterfall before meeting a vehicle track, which is followed north-westwards, climbing the hillsides to

The inn at Tan Hill.

The Butter Tubs.

East Stonesdale Farm, where there are fine views over Keld.

STONESDALE MOOR

The route continues northwards above the valley of West Stonesdale to reach the rough pastures of Black Moor. Beyond the isolated spartan dwellings of Frith Lodge and High Frith, the valley becomes increasingly desolate - so different from the pastoral charms of Swaledale.

After crossing Mould Gill and Lad Gill the rutted track climbs north-eastwards over the dull expanses of Stonesdale Moor, passing an old quarry and the remnants of several disused coal mines en route. Tan Hill's inn comes into view after a convergence of tracks at GR 897061. The stark building is truly remote and is claimed to be the highest public house in England at 1732 ft (527m) above sea level. The shiny black and yellow Theakston's sign promises the weary traveller a good pint of best Yorkshire ale too! It is a grand place to spend the night.

HAWES TO TAN HILL
Alternative Route via the Butter Tubs and Punchard Moor

The badly eroded ascent of Great Shunner Fell can be avoided by climbing Pike Hill and dropping down into Swaledale via the Butter Tubs Pass. It would have been good to have continued the route over Lovely Seat and Rogan's Seat, but unfortunately both number among the growing list of peaks considered 'out of bounds to

walkers'. Common land does not mean there is a freedom to roam in North Yorkshire.

HAWES

After following the Hardraw lane out of the village, the route traverses fields north-eastwards to Sedbusk. This peaceful hamlet lies beneath the limestone terraces of Pike Hill, the southern bastion of Abbotside Common.

PIKE HILL

A walled track known as Shutt Lane climbs north-eastwards across the lofty fields of Sedbusk High pasture. It is left at GR 888915 for an obvious path heading for a gap in the limestone crags. Once on the plateau's edge head in a westerly direction . Occasional cairns highlight the way. The views are similar to those on the ascent of Great Shunner Fell but those eastwards down the length of Wensleydale are superior.

BUTTER TUBS

Although it will be tempting to continue the climb over peat-hagged terrain to the summit of Lovely Seat, it is more prudent to follow the bridleway, which descends to the high country lane linking Hawes and Thwaite. The lane climbs to the Butter Tubs Pass, a high and wild saddle between the barren moorlands of Great Shunner Fell and Lovely Seat. The place gets its name from a group of potholes that lie either side of the road. The shafts with protruding limestone pillars are up to 80ft deep.

THWAITE AND MUKER

Beyond the Butter Tubs the road arcs into Swaledale with fine views down the length of the verdant valley.

The official Pennine Way is briefly encountered at Thwaite before continuing down the lane to Muker. For those wishing to stay the night there is a camp-site at Usha Gap Bridge and a good inn at the heart of the village.

A walled track leads north-westwards out of the village towards Kisdon Hill. Leave it at GR 908987 for a footpath doubling back to cross the River Swale on the Ramps Holme footbridge (not named on 1:50000 maps). A riverside path now heads northwards with the ruins of Crackpot Hall high on the hillside ahead and the craggy defile of Swinner Gill to its right.

SWINNER GILL

The path enters Swinner Gill, crossing the stream at GR 911008. It then climbs the grassy hillslopes to reach a well defined track leading to the old lead mine workings beneath Swinner Gill Kirk. The area is studded by ruined barracks and slag heaps.

From the mines a narrow path climbs by the north banks of East Grain to reach the heather moors, where it joins a wide, flinted track. At the highest point many will be tempted to head northwards on the track to Rogan's Seat but, again, we are thwarted by the interests of grouse shooting and so we continue eastwards across an area of tips and shafts of the Lownathwaite Lead Mines. As the track turns southwards it is left for a path descending through heather to the north of North Hush. It then veers left (north-east) into the depths of Gunnerside Gill, at its confluence with Blind Gill (GR 937018). The valley is littered with the scars of the now defunct lead mining industry.

GUNNERSIDE GILL

Gunnerside Gill is crossed via a slabbed bridge to Blakethwaite Smelt Mill, an impressive ruin with fine archways. A zigzag path climbs from the ruins to meet a prominent track which is followed southwards, climbing steadily across a series of hushes. Shortly before reaching Bunton Crushing Mill (GR 940013) our route climbs out of Gunnerside on a rough course up Bunton Hush (not named on 1:50000 maps). At the top it meets a miners' road continuing eastwards across gravelly wastes to look down on the shallow valley of

Lead mines in Gunnerside Gill.

Passing the waterfalls of Great Punchard Gill near Great Punchard Head.

Hard Level Gill. This is the point where we rejoin the East Dales Loop (see appendix).

PUNCHARD MOOR

The track is abandoned at a pile of stones adjacent to a track coming in from the right from the ruins of Moor House. The bridleway is sketchy at first but if you look across the moors to the north you will see it as a grassy channel through the heather. Do not lose sight of it as it is the key to the difficult part of an otherwise fool-

proof route. From the pile of stones at the junction of tracks descend on the sketchy, cairned path through heather to ford a stream. A grassy ramp then climbs past the spoil heaps of Friarfold Rake (not named on 1:50000 maps).

Beyond here the route is more prominent and we follow the grassy track seen earlier to a fence-corner high on the moors. The fence is followed north-north-westwards before you cross it via a small gate. The path continues in the same direction over the lofty

for thirty yards before doubling back along a Land-rover track. This peters out to become a path heading north-westwards over the rough grasslands of West Moor.

WILLIAM GILL AND TAN HILL

On Scollit Side the moorland becomes more heathery and a line of grouse butts can be seen below. Splendid views open up to the head of Arkengarthdale and the shallow depression of the Greta Valley. Beyond the sombre low moors of the Stainmore Forest the moorland swells to high mountain scenery, reaching its zenith on Cross Fell. On a clear day you will be able to pick out the white radome on Great Dun Fell, while the many cairns of Nine Standards Rigg appear on the western horizon.

After passing a tall cairn the path drops down into William Gill just to the south of a ruined dwelling. Cross the gill and follow it to the right to the ruins. For those who want to stop at the inn at Tan Hill a bridle-way (very sketchy underfoot) traverses the open moorland. A wireless mast close to Tan Hill acts as a good guide, once the Mirk Fell ridge has been surmounted.

Those wishing to press on can follow a good path along William Gill to the Tan Hill Road at The Disputes. Turn left here to old Bowes Road (GR 929075), a stony lane leading to the main Pennine Way route a mile short of Sleightholme.

grasslands of Punchard Moor, with the pasture-decked valley of Arkengarthdale appearing beyond the barren slopes of Great Pinseat. On approaching the ravine of Great Punchard Gill it veers left, revealing some lovely waterfalls. Narrow sheeptracks now traverse a reedy area, climbing to the streamside lead-mining ruin of Punchard Head, at the termination of the Great Punchard Gill track.

The gill is forded close to the ruins (the old bridge has been demolished). Turn right along the stony lane

ROUTE FILE

Maps	OS Landranger (1:50000) Nos 98 and 92 or Outdoor Leisure Map (1:25000) No. 30 'Yorkshire Dales North & Central'	
Distance and time Official Way Alternative Routes to Tan Hill to Bowes	16 miles (26km) 19 miles (30km) 25 miles (40km)	9 hours 11 hours 13 hours
Terrain	Long gruelling climb to Great Shunner followed by easy descent into Swaledale. Good easy paths to Keld and across rough moorland to Tan Hill. The alternative route is a mixture of very wild moorland (Punchard Moor) combined with easy tracks and lanes.	
Accommodation	Youth Hostel at Keld. Camp-sites and B&Bs at Thwaite, Keld and Muker; inns at Tan Hill and Muker.	
Shops	At Muker.	
Tourist Information	43, Galgate, Barnard Castle, County Durham. DL12 8EL. Tel. 0833 690909	

Above: Approaching William Gill from Great Scollit Hill. Below: The ruins in William Gill.

9

OVER EMPTY MOORS TO TEESDALE

Tan Hill to Middleton-in-Teesdale

Here we leave the dales of Yorkshire for the less celebrated moors of County Durham. This is not one of the Pennine Way's most spectacular days and many will understandably have the urge to pass through as quickly and painlessly as possible.

You start by squelching through the marshes surrounding Frumming Beck and continue in subdued fashion to Sleightholme, where travellers who want nearby accommodation are offered an alternative - 'the Bowes Loop'. The more direct route via God's Bridge is scenically superior if only for the inclusion of the wild heather moors of Ravock. Both routes rejoin by the reservoirs of Baldersdale. After crossing the Upper Lune Valley and scaling hills to the north, the landscape softens and we descend to verdant Teesdale at Middleton.

Sombre though the moors are, there is a sense of drama in the region, whether it be the reminders of Dickens Dotheboys Hall in Bowes, Hannah Hauxwell's old farm in remote Lunedale or simply the wide, untamed landscapes and the undulating uplands of Ravock, Goldsborough and Baldersdale.

I have offered no alternatives on this section. Any other possibilities are hampered by lack of available access to the likes of Mickle Fell (firing ranges) and Stainmore Forest (grouse moors). Happily there is little erosion hereabouts for few day-walkers set foot in the area. The moors will belong to you.

The heather-clad Ravock Moor.

TAN HILL TO MIDDLETON
The Official Route

TAN HILL AND SLEIGHTHOLME MOOR

The view northwards from Tan Hill is even more barren and desolate than the previous landscapes of Stonesdale. The dark, bare peatlands of Sleightholme Moor decline gradually to the depression of Frumming Beck. Further north the hillsides rise to Bowes Moor, with the more distinguished profile of Mickle Fell on the skyline.

The way beyond Tan Hill begins from the east of the inn and is a little sketchy in places although infrequent cairns aid route-finding. To make matters worse the peat-ridden terrain is spongy at best, but is more often sodden and miry. The path descends to the northern banks of Frumming Beck, which it accompanies to GR 916082 where a crossing is made. The numerous fordings of feeder streams make the going arduous until a vehicle track is met close to the confluence of Frumming and Sleightholme Becks. The track is then followed to its junction with the Sleightholme Moor Road. This flinted track leads north-eastwards past Sleightholme Farm, whose buildings are set in a

verdant hollow and are not seen until the final approaches.

Beyond the farm the road is metalled. Leave the road for a path that traverses fields to the left, heading for the sandy crags of Bog Scar. Sleightholme Beck is crossed via a footbridge at the foot of the scar. A grassy track then zigzags to the cliff-tops, which are followed north-eastwards parallel to the beck and adjacent to a dry-stone wall. The path crosses to the other side of the wall via a gate close to Trough Heads Farm and here there is a divergence of the official Pennine Way routes. The 'Bowes Loop' alternative is used by those who seek nearby accommodation (Bowes village is 3 miles away). The more direct main route crosses Wytham and Cotherstone Moor to Baldersdale, where they both meet again.

THE OFFICIAL ROUTE VIA GOD'S BRIDGE AND RAVOCK CASTLE

SLEIGHTHOLME

From the wall the route traverses heathland to the enclosure's northern wall, which is followed westwards

Sleightholme Beck north of Tan Hill.

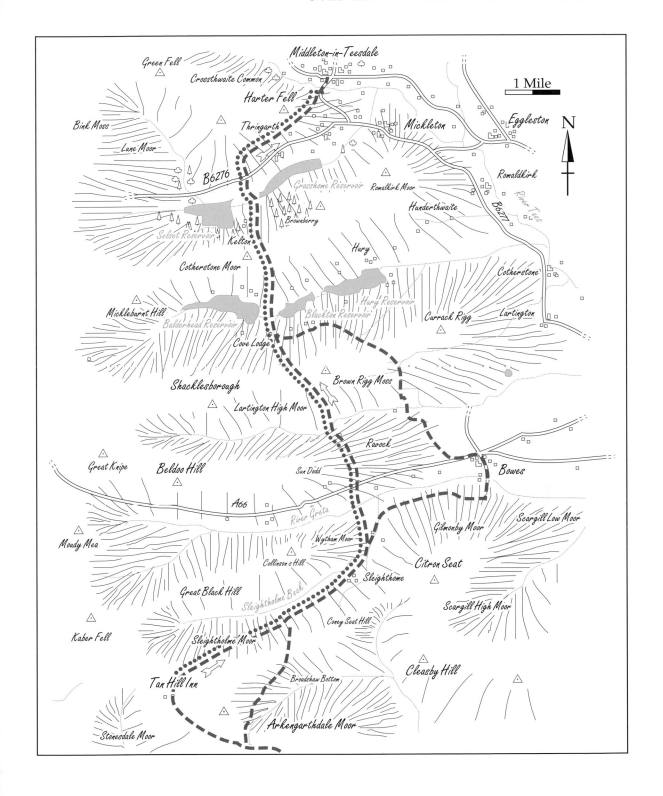

Above: Looking southwards across Race Yate, Cotherstone Moor on the main route.
Below: Crossing the moors of Ravock, north of Bowes with the lonely ruins of Ravock Castle crumbling into the reeds.

God's Bridge on the main route.

for a hundred yards and crossed via a ladder stile. The path then descends across meadowland towards the River Greta. The gritstone of the moorlands has now been briefly replaced by limestone and the riverbed is usually dry because the stream flows beneath the surface. A huge slab of rock spans a deep pool in the river bed to form God's Bridge, a natural phenomenon that has been used for centuries by farmers and drovers alike. On the opposite bank of the river is a well-preserved lime kiln. The path passes to the east of it before climbing past a farmhouse and dismantled railway to reach the busy A66 road 3 miles west of Bowes.

RAVOCK
After risking life and limb crossing the busy dual carriageway the route continues northwards past Pasture End Farm and by a wall before continuing on a narrow, sparsely-cairned track that crosses the heather and bracken-clad moors of Ravock. Ravock Castle is little more than a pile of stones and is almost certainly the remains of a modest shepherd's hut.

Beyond the 'castle' the route descends to Deepdale Beck, which is crossed by a concrete footbridge. The path now continues by a dry-stone wall over undulating grassy flanks to Race Yate Rigg where a stile crosses the ridge fence. First views into Baldersdale appear

with the massive Balderhead Reservoir dominating the scene.

BALDERSDALE
A narrow track descends Cotherstone Moor, a wild tract of undulating wilderness covered with pale moor grass and dark reeds. On the descent, the smaller Blackton Reservoir comes into view, surrounded by verdant farmlands. The path emerges at a narrow metalled lane, which is followed briefly to Clove Lodge. Beyond a gate to the left of the farm a path descends by a wall across meadows to Blackton Bridge, which lies in the shadow of the huge earth-fill dam of the Balderhead Reservoir.

The bridge is crossed and a track veers left to pass Birk Hat Farm, now part of a nature reserve but once home to Hannah Hauxwell. A newly laid gravel path climbs pastureland to reach the road north of another farm, High Birk Hat. Staggered slightly to the left along the road, the continuing path climbs to the left of a wall across the rough reedy pastures of Hazelgarth Rigg.

LUNEDALE
On reaching the ridge there is a feeling of *déjà vu* for ahead is Lunedale, the twin of Baldersdale with its three reservoirs. To the right is a recent plantation of

Above: Low Birk Hat Farm, Baldersdale next to a half-empty Blackton Reservoir. The cottage was formerly Hannah Hauxwell's home.

spruce and a couple of curious towers that mark the line of a tunnel, linking the reservoirs of Lunedale and Baldersdale.

The route now descends into the valley opposite How Farm. The line of the Pennine Way marked on current maps is no longer feasible and the walker is forced to use the road descending to the Grassholme Reservoir, crossing it via a five-arched stone bridge. In times of drought an old twin-arched bridge is revealed which is, at present, remarkably intact.

Bowes Castle and village.

HARTER FELL

After going through the yard of Grassholme Farm a rutted track begins the climb across meadowland to reach the Brough-Middleton road. The route continues on the other side along a lane, passing to the left of both Wythes Hill and Colin Hill Farms. The walled track terminates at a small stream to the north of the latter and the well-waymarked route climbs north-eastwards over rougher pastures to Harter Fell. The views are steadily improving and glimpses of Teesdale widening. Some interesting ruins dot the hillside to the right above Greengates Quarry. Slightly further afield is Kirkcarrion. Here gaunt pine trees crown a rounded grassy peak.

As the ridge is gained, suddenly Teesdale is revealed beneath your feet. The subdued mood that you have almost certainly been feeling of late will be gone. Middleton lies snug by the riverside beneath emerald hill slopes. Further north are real mountains - the first since leaving the Yorkshire Dales.

MIDDLETON-IN-TEESDALE

The descent over lush sheep-shorn grass is easy. After turning right on reaching the Holwick lane, the main road to the village is reached. The few not wanting or not having the time to visit Middleton will turn right on the lane by the cattle market but most will continue across the bridge over the Tees into the village where supplies can be replenished (the local grocer sells really good ice cream).

The BOWES LOOP
An Official Alternative
From Sleightholme to Baldersdale

Middleton-in-Teesdale from Harter Fell.

SLEIGHTHOLME MOOR AND BOWES

For those urgently seeking accommodation, Bowes offers a good choice.

Pennine Wayers are offered an official alternative, 'The Bowes Loop'. In my opinion much of this variation is inferior to the more direct line via God's Bridge and Ravock and involves some road walking.

The loop begins from Trough Heads Farm and continues by the wall on the right until it meets a track from West Mellwaters Farm. This is followed eastwards to the larger East Mellwaters Farm, where there is a camp-site. After passing close to the cowsheds the path closely follows a stone wall before veering left across fields close to the tree-lined River Greta. Sleightholme Beck is recrossed *en route* to the next farm, Lady Mires. From here a lane leads eastwards to meet a country road at Gilmonby a few hundred yards south of Bowes village.

Bowes itself is a spartan place, once inhabited by the Romans. The Norman castle, said to have been visited by King John, lies in ruins which tower over the surrounding cottages. Another distinguished visitor to Bowes was Charles Dickens and Wickford Squeers's Dotheboys Hall School is reputed to be the large terraced building at the western end of the village.

TUTE HILL

After passing through the village the road leads over the main A66 dual carriageway and heads northwards past the awful dereliction of a Ministry of Defence site. 'Keep out - poison gas signs', now fading, are a reminder of its unsavoury past. At the termination of the road by West Stoney Keld Farm, a rutted vehicle track leads across a field past the ruins of Levy Pool Farm to Deepdale Beck, which is forded before tackling the wastelands of Hazelgill Rigg. The way under-

foot is unclear, being little more than a narrow sheep-track starting slightly to the east of the ford and heading northwards across rough moorland. After crossing Hazelgill Beck the track veers right through bracken to reach a gate in a wall separating walkers from more military land - this time a firing range.

GOLDSBOROUGH

The wall is then followed northwards, passing through another gate before continuing along a sketchy track which bears left (west-north-west) towards the distinctive crags of Goldsborough. The crags are circumvented to the south and west before reaching a country lane, which is followed westwards to meet the main route at Clove Lodge south of the Baldersdale Reservoirs.

ROUTE FILE		
Maps	OS Landranger (1:50000) No. 92 or Outdoor Leisure Map (1:25000) Nos 30 'Yorkshire Dales North & Central' and 31 'Teesdale' would be useful.	
Distance and time Official Way Via Bowes Loop	16 miles (26km) 20 miles (32km)	9 hours 11 hours
Terrain	Much featureless moorland punctuated by paths and tracks over isolated farmland. A little road walking on the Bowes Loop.	
Accommodation	Youth hostel in Baldersdale; B&Bs, inns and camp-sites at Middleton; inns, B&Bs and a camp-site at Bowes (on Bowes Loop).	
Shops	At Middleton-in-Teesdale and also Bowes (on Bowes Loop).	
Tourist Information	43, Galgate, Barnard Castle, County Durham. DL12 8EL. Tel. 0833 690909.	

10

FIRST TASTE OF THE NORTH PENNINES

Middleton-in-Teesdale to Dufton

In its upper reaches the Tees is, in my opinion, England's finest river. It provides a wonderful appetizer and delightfully easy stroll before the slog up the empty moors of the high North Pennine Hills. Around Middleton, the river meanders relatively calmly through verdant pastures but, once past the hamlet of Newbiggin, it becomes increasingly boisterous, forming waterfalls, the most spectacular being High Force and Cauldron Snout.

The Pennine Way would not feel quite right without climbing the highest peak, Cross Fell. However, if conditions are appalling and unlikely to change, I have provided a low-level route via the Cow Green Reservoir to the South Tyne hamlet of Garrigill. This would also save one day.

Those who make the slog up the bare moors are rewarded by the finest single spectacle the North Pennines have to offer - High Cup, a huge amphitheatre of basaltic crags.

Descending to Dufton is illogical but the high peaks between High Cup and Knock Fell form part of a grouse moor and Site of Special Scientific Interest with no rights of way. The descent is, however, an easy one and is accompanied by delightful views westward over the wide Eden Valley to the Lakeland Fells. There's also the promise of a welcoming pint at the Stag Inn.

Opposite: Cauldron Snout.　　　　　*Below: Heading west alongside Maize Beck towards High Cup Nick.*　(Photo: Phil Iddon)

MIDDLETON-IN-TEESDALE
To DUFTON
The Official Route

MIDDLETON IN TEESDALE

After previous wanderings over dull and marshy moorlands, the spirits will be uplifted by the promise of fine scenery in the Teesdale and North Pennine regions. Middleton's bridge over the Tees is recrossed and a Pennine Way sign (GR 946253) directs walkers to a cart track. This leads westwards before an obvious path continues high above the south banks of the river, which meanders in the plain below. The surrounding pastoral landscape has a spaciousness that is special to this part of the country. Most of the scattered farmhouses and dwellings are whitewashed and stand out against the verdant lower hillsides which, in spring and summer, are laden with numerous wild flowers. The fells, in contrast, are stark and bare, smooth-profiled and rounded.

LOW AND HIGH FORCE

At GR 917266, the path descends from high fields through woodland to the banks of the Tees crossing a streamlet en route via a wooden footbridge. The riverbank is then followed through wooded glens. By Wynch Bridge the scene has been transformed further. The Tees has gained power and rushes over a faulted rocky platform in torrents and cataracts. It is now crowded by craggy bluffs and cliffs, and trees thickly

Above: The Tees plummets seventy feet through a nick in the dolerite cliffs at High Force, said to be the largest waterfalls in England. Below: Walking along the banks of the River Tees near Middleton. Opposite Page: Low Force.

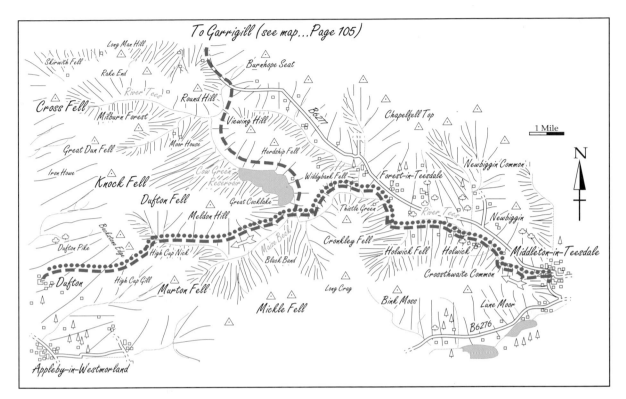

To Garrigill (see map...Page 105)

line the valleysides. The power of this section of the Tees culminates in Low Force.

At Holwick Head Bridge the way has been 'improved'. I understand the need to protect the countryside from the erosion now taking place but the cinder footpaths that follow belong to an urban park not a rural scene such as this. Soon the thundering roar of High Force can be heard. It remains hidden however, until the last moment when the path leads through shrubs to the edge of a huge dark cliff forming the river's southern bank. The river, which has been babbling over a rocky bed, suddenly finds its course restricted. It thrashes through a breach in the dark dolerite crags in a white plume before tumbling over perpendicular cliffs into a huge deep pool below. Although not the tallest at seventy feet, High Force is regarded as the largest waterfall in England. Some have said that it is not as

Above: Cauldron Snout and falcon Clints from Birkdale. Below: Heading for Widdybank Farm.

spectacular since the dam at Cow Green was constructed.

An unpleasant surprise lurks around the corner beyond High Force - a large quarrying works. The factory adds a grey gloom to the sombre lonely heather moors and, although it provides employment for the local population, the cost to the landscape is high indeed!

CRONKLEY
From Pasture Foot, the path rises steeply on a bracken-

covered knoll before veering north at a Pennine Way sign. After a slight depression preceding High Crag, a descent amongst rocky outcrops is made to Cronkley Farm. A farm road across green meadows then leads to Cronkley Bridge where the Tees is rejoined. Cross the bridge and follow the riverbank. A short distance upstream there is a confluence and the Tees alters course to flow at the foot of Cronkley Scar, which will be seen to better advantage later. The watercourse now being followed is Langden Beck. When I was last here, a myriad of wild flowers bedecked the path's verge and the scene was ablaze with colour.

WIDDYBANK
If urgent shelter is required for the night, a decision has to be made at Saur Hill Bridge (not marked on 1:50000 maps) at GR 854303. Accommodation is available at Langden Beck village. To get there turn right by the nearside of the bridge. This leads to the youth hostel and inn.

For those who wish to continue to Dufton, the bridge is crossed. An approach road then leads to Saur Hill Farm (not named on 1:50000 maps, and incorrectly named Sayer Hill on 1:25000 maps). From here a path traverses fields to rejoin the banks of the Tees north of Cronkley Scar. These dark crags and the inhospitable moorland at their feet contrast starkly with the green fields surrounding the white-washed buildings of Widdybank Farm, which lies directly ahead.

The riverbank is left briefly to join a stony cart track leading to Widdybank Farm. Here well-earned refreshments such as tea and cake can be purchased. Bed and breakfast is also available all year round - a welcome break, for the distance between here and Dufton is still 12 miles (19.2km)!

Beyond Widdybank the valley narrows and crags fringe both flanks. The riverside path arcs gently to the right and the terrain becomes rougher. To the east are the desolate slopes of Mickle Fell, the highest peak in Durham. Unfortunately it is out of bounds for the fell-walker because it is part of the vast Ministry of Defence firing range.

The path continues over a bouldery course beneath Falcon Clints, an escarpment with steep slopes of heather interspersed with crag and scree.

CAULDRON SNOUT AND COW GREEN

At the northern extremities of Falcon Clints, a stream from the high Pennines joins the lively waters of the Tees. This is Maize Beck, a stream that will later guide our course through some of the loneliest country in the whole of England. The tranquillity of the scene is soon disturbed by the explosive cascades of Cauldron Snout, aptly named for this is a great white foaming cauldron. One can only be amazed at the awesome power of the river as it smashes and rumbles relentlessly over the dolerite rocks that confine and channel its course.

After scrambling over rocks by the side of the waterfall, the illusion that these waters are untamed is shattered for there ahead is a huge concrete dam - one flick of a switch and the water stops! The dam contains Cow Green Reservoir, built amid tremendous controversy (*See* box.)

Beneath the dam a bridge spans the river. A decision has to be made whether to follow the official route to Dufton or steal a day and make directly for Alston via the South Tyne Valley and Garrigill.

MAIZE BECK

The route to Dufton crosses the bridge and follows a track southwards. A slight detour to the edge of the embankment to the left will offer lofty retrospective views of Cauldron Snout and the River Tees, which resembles a shimmering serpent basking in the shade of Falcon Clints. Continuing past the old farm of Birkdale, the path descends to cross Grains Beck, a tributary of Maize Beck. From here the slog up vast and lonely moors to High Cup Nick begins.

A tall cairn on slopes above guides the walker to some old mine workings known as the Moss Shop. In

Heading west towards High Cup Nick between Moss Shop and Maize Beck (Photo: Phil Iddon)

Above: High Cup.
Below: Dufton Village.

harder times the local miners would have had to sleep here five days a week - probably in damp conditions sleeping on lice-infested sacks.

The trek continues over peatlands before a sketchy path descends to the banks of Maize Beck, which flows on a bed of limestone from high hills on the horizon. Now the peat is replaced by the short grass that is synonymous with limestone scenery. When I was last here the beck was nearly dry but often, I have heard, it can be swift-flowing and dangerous to cross. Ford it here if it is safe and continue along its southern banks - if not continue to GR 748271 where there is a foot-bridge.

HIGH CUP

As Maize Beck turns northwards to be lost in the dank and sombre slopes of Dufton Fell, the main route continues westwards on a good firm path. It follows a line of stone cairns over the grassy expanses of High Cup Plain. On reaching the edge of the plain your spirits will be uplifted for spread before you is one of England's most spectacular mountain views - High Cup! An enormous scoop has been scoured from the hillsides to form an amphitheatre, fringed by dolerite cliffs and strangely isolated pillars. Grey screes, which have fallen from these high cliffs, exaggerate the symmetry of the smooth, grassy slopes, which plummet to High Cup Gill Beck far below. The silvery stream meanders out of the hollow into the vast flatlands of the Eden Valley. In the distance, if atmospheric conditions allow, the Lakeland Fells are discernible. Blencathra and the High Street Range are particularly prominent.

Although it is tempting to stay on the high ridge, the official Pennine Way descends to Dufton from here. It skirts the northern edge of High Cup beneath the flanks of Narrowgate Beacon, fording a couple of tumbling gills en route. A descent is then made to Peeping Hill and an old quarry before entering enclosed farmland on slopes high above the Eden Valley.

DUFTON

The walled cart track that follows is very welcome after the toils of the day and makes the final descent towards Dufton much easier. Although one is always searching for the hidden village among the fields below, the views ahead are dominated by the conical Dufton Pike. Beyond Bow Hall, the cart track becomes a narrow tarmac lane leading to the main road south of Dufton. The centre is charming. Pleasant stone cottages surround a wide green partially shaded by tall, proud horse chestnuts, with Dufton Pike forming a backdrop. There is a good inn, a camp-site, a youth hostel and some bed and breakfast accommodation to help you take a break before that slog to the highest Pennine Hill, Cross Fell.

COW GREEN

Cow Green slept for centuries. This peaceful backwater of Upper Teesdale had been a remote farming and lead-mining community. It had long been known that the area was of great interest to botanists for teams had often made pilgrimages here in furtherance of their science. Even when the site was declared a nature reserve in 1963 and the people from the Nature Conservancy Council shackled the farmers' activities a status quo was reached and they learned to live in relative harmony. The peace was shattered, however, in the mid-sixties, when the ever-thirsty appetite of industrial Teesside demanded that a new reservoir be constructed. Cow Green was chosen.

Conservationists were up in arms. Letters were sent to *The Times*; scientists from all over the world protested that the site was just too valuable. A public enquiry was set up.

What made Cow Green so special? It is believed to be the harsh climate and the presence of sugar limestone, a rock that has been baked by the intrusion of molten whin sill, the other predominant rock of the region. Behaving and looking like sand, its soils support a multitude of species, including blue gentian, dog violet, thyme, harebell, shrubby cinquefoil, primrose, and spring sandwort. The Teesdale Violet only grows on Widdybank Fell. Tracts of juniper also helped the survival of a large bird population. The site had one famous view - the Teesdale Wheel, where the Tees flowed in a huge circle before plummeting down Cauldron Snout.

In the end all this counted for nought. Peace has returned to the valley but, since 1971, it has lain beneath a sheet of water headed by a huge concrete dam. Fortunately scientists and volunteers were allowed access to the site before flooding in order to remove specimens of the rare species and replant them above the water-line. Sadly, no one will see the Teesdale Wheel again and a wild and wonderful valley has been desecrated.

Cow Green Reservoir from the stony track north towards Garrigill.

COW GREEN TO GARRIGILL
An Alternative Route

COW GREEN

At the bridge above Cauldron Snout, a metalled lane leads north-eastwards past the huge dam and thence close to the shores of the lake to the visitor car park. The stony track that continues north-westwards heads over lonely moors close to the reservoir's eastern shores before reaching the Middleton to Alston road at GR 784354. I had considered including a route across the rough moorland which links the right of way at Tyne Head crossing Metalband Hill (between GR 780330 and 761340). The path would then lead to Garrigill including a quiet stretch of country lane. However the presence of grouse butts made me hesitant for grouse-shooting men are no respecters of the 'freedom to roam' principle. It is also at the heart of the Nature Reserve - and these people are also no respecters of that same principle (see their notices on the fells). In conclusion I thought that the recommended route should follow the Alston road for two miles to Ash Gill. The road is one of the highest in England and passes over empty heathland below Burnhope Seat where it reaches an altitude of 1962 ft (598m).

GARRIGILL

The road is abandoned for a footpath that descends on the southern edge of the craggy gorge of Ash Gill, close to the perimeter of a small conifer plantation. The waterfalls of Ashgill Force are well worth seeing when in spate. A footbridge allows the crossing of the stream below the falls and the way is now north-westwards across fields, parallel to the South Tyne, which flows through the lush meadows below.

After passing many farmhouses, turn right at Loaning Head into an access road leading into Garrigill. This lovely former lead-mining village has a large green and a good pub. Many people pass through Garrigill without seeing the river which flows lazily in silence and seclusion in a deep, dark, leafy gorge.

For the map and routes to Alston see the next chapter.

ROUTE FILE

Maps	OS.Landranger (1:50000) Nos 92 'Barnard Castle' and 91 'Appleby-in- Westmorland' Outdoor Leisure Map (1:25000) No 31 'Teesdale' would be useful.
Distance and time Official Way	17 miles (28km) 10 hours
Alternative Route to Alston	20 miles (32km) 12 hours
Terrain	Easy riverside paths to Widdybank Fell then going gets rougher, traversing high moorland to High Cup, where good paths and tracks descend to Dufton. Although longer the Cow Green route direct to Alston is easier. It stays on good tracks north of the reservoir and on riverside paths from Garrigill to Alston.
Accommodation	Youth hostel at Langdon Beck. Youth hostel, inn, B&B and camp-site at Dufton. On the alternative Cow Green route there are B&Bs and an inn at Garrigill and also a youth hostel, inns, B&Bs and a camp-site at Alston.
Shops	At Middleton-in-Teesdale, Garrigill and Alston.
Tourist Information	Moot Hall, Boroughgate, Appleby-in Westmorland, Cumbria, CA16 6XD. Tel. 07683 52546.

11

SCALING THE HIGHEST PENNINE TOPS
Dufton to Alston

The price for descending to Dufton must now be paid and the struggle back to the high Pennine ridge is a hard one, perhaps the hardest of the whole journey!

After a brief walk through the fields of the Eden valley, the flanks of Knock Fell are climbed to gain the ridge a wild place at the edge of a vast area of wilderness stretching to the banks of the infant Tees.

The masts of the military radar and weather station are perched like aliens on Great Dun Fell. The urge will be to pass them quickly in order to reach Cross Fell. This peer of the Pennines is the highest point of the Pennine Way. Its firm summit terrain offers a fine platform to view a wide panorama of the Lakeland Fells, which are seen across the Eden Valley

The loneliness and expanse of these mountains is best experienced on the descent to the South Tyne Valley. The path meanders through vast, bare, undulating moorland divided by streams, now called burns, in a landscape bereft of the scales of time and distance. In silence and probably in weariness, one can contemplate that piping hot meal or cool drink at the George and Dragon before tackling that final stretch via the riverbanks of the South Tyne to the cobbled streets and stone-built terraces of Alston.

Looking from the southern edge of the Cross Fell plateau to the radar station on Great Dun Fell.

DUFTON TO ALSTON
The Official Route

DUFTON

Dufton's conical Pike lifts our eyes to the hills. It must be hoped that the weather is clement for Cross Fell, at 2930ft (893m) and subject to that 'Helm Wind', is the last place we want a lack of visibility.

A farm track from GR 691251 strikes north-eastwards with Dufton Pike directly ahead. After about a hundred yards so it is abandoned for a track that heads north for Coatsike Farm. Here it continues across green pastures beneath the Pike's western slopes. The landscape is parcelled by dry-stone walls and broad-leaved woodland. A descent is made to the wooded glade of Great Rundale Beck. The stream is crossed by an old stone clapper bridge and a straight green road is then followed, climbing to the edge of the stone-strewn moorland beneath Brownber Hill.

KNOCK FELL

Swindale Beck is crossed and the climb proceeds on a cairned track north-eastwards across stony slopes towards the high ridge. On the horizon Great Dun Fell's alien white dome and masts always command attention. Although ugly and unwelcome, they act as magnets to those who are impatient to reach the high fells. The craggy gash of Swindale Beck maintains interest during the long climb and there are reminders of bygone industry at Knock Hush, a watercourse artificially constructed by breaching the dam of a temporary reservoir. The rushing waters would then strip the vegetation to the subsoil, which could be inspected for traces of lead.

Eventually the ridge is gained at Knock Fell, whose flat, grassy summit is scattered with a profusion of cairns including the splendid square and squat Knock Old Man. Views from the fell reveal a stunning contrast in landscapes. To the west are the fertile plains of the Vale of Eden while, in the opposite direction, mile upon mile of sullen dark rolling hills stretch to the skyline.

GREAT DUN FELL

The way ahead is northwards to Great Dun Fell but first there is a slight descent across peaty slopes to a depression where the narrow metalled radar station approach road is met. This can be used to gain the summit but the official Pennine Way goes to the east of

Passing the Knock Old Man, a huge cairn on the summit of Knock Fell, which is the first peak of the day.

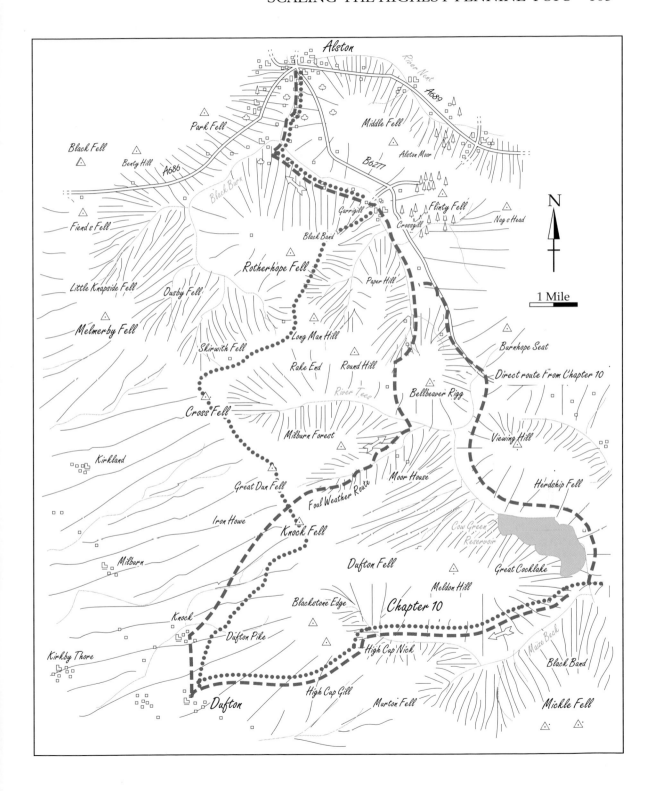

On the high ridge near Tees Head with the massif of Cross Fell ahead.

it, crossing Dunfell Hush before climbing north-west-wards behind those horrid monstrosities! In views to the south-east, across the vast empty moors of the Milburn Forest, it is possible to see down to Cow Green Reservoir.

Most walkers will want to pass the station quickly and head for the next summit, Little Dun Fell, which divides us from the distinctive flat-topped Cross Fell. Rapid progress is made on firm dry turf and we are soon standing on the narrow peak.

CROSS FELL

Cross Fell's massive grassy flanks are fringed with blue-grey boulders and scree and totally dominate and restrict all views. The firm terrain we have recently enjoyed is interrupted at Tees Head, in the depression between Little Dun Fell and Cross Fell. Here, in an area darkened by peat hags, the Northern Pennines give birth to the River Tees, and like all river sources it is very marshy underfoot. Soon the terrain becomes firm once more and the climb begins up the stony southern slopes past a series of cairns to the top of Cross Fell.

The mountain was once known as Fiends' Fell because evil spirits were said to congregate here. An early Christian, St Paulinus, was supposed to have

erected a cross on the summit and held a mass to exor-cize them. The grassy plateau is vast and strewn with boulders. It has a good stone shelter (much needed on windy days) and a concrete trig. point. Panoramas on a clear day are uninterrupted and spectacular, with views to the north opening up to reveal the high but seldom frequented grouse moors of Gilderdale Forest. I have read little about these hills but paths are few and shoot-ing huts are many. I imagine they are very private.

Beyond Gilderdale the vista widens to encompass the Scottish Borders region across the Solway Firth. The western prospect over Eden is exquisite and one can spend hours gazing at favourite Lake District peaks. The High Street range seems very close and the individual paths are sometimes discernible. If atmos-pheric conditions are clear, you will be able to see the Cheviots - an itinerary near journey's end!

The initial descent from Cross Fell can be confus-ing, especially in mist, for the tracks are indistinct. After taking a north-north-westerly course, aided by the occasional cairn, to the northern bouldered fringe of the summit plateau, a north-westerly course leads to a well defined east-west track on a col between Cross Fell and the unnamed hill marked with a spot height 786. If in doubt about the terrain hereabouts use your compass rather than your instincts because the scale of

Descending to Greg's Hut from Cross Fell.

the place disorientates the senses in this vast hillscape - and one burn looks much like another among these featureless fells.

GREG'S HUT

Turn right along the track. This was once a corpse road, along which Garrigill's dead were carried to consecrated ground at Kirkland in the Eden Valley. Half a mile to the east, in total isolation, is an old stone cottage, Greg's Hut. It was restored by the Mountain Bothies Association to offer shelter for weary travellers. If you use the hut make sure you clean up afterwards so that others can enjoy their stay.

The path now enters an area littered by the debris, shafts and spoil heaps of the old disused lead mines. The ground is covered with purple crystalline pebbles of fluorspar or Blue John, a waste product of the mining.

Continuing past the mines, the track veers northwards, passing Long Man Hill and Pikeman Hill. Views of the green swathes of the South Tyne Valley become wider as the long descent draws to a close. At GR 729394 the official route abandons the track to cut a corner but it does not exist underfoot and, in practice, no time will be saved.

GARRIGILL

The appearance of the cottages of Garrigill heralds a

Approaching Garrigill.

(Photo: Phil Iddon)

CROSS FELL LEAD MINES

On the traverse of the high Northern Pennines one cannot help but notice the evidence of extensive mining on the fells - the artificial hushes on Knock Fell and Great Dun Fell and the shafts, debris and relics on the descent to Garrigill. The area is rich in lead, silver, iron, zinc and copper - all have been mined here.

It was lead that brought prosperity to the region. The Romans were first to discover it but their diggings were not extensive. Mining was resumed by the Earls of Derwentwater, but in 1716, the last Earl, Jame,s was executed on Tower Hill for his part in the Jacobite rebellions. His lands were granted to the Greenwich Hospital who still own them to this day.

Horizontal passages (levels), some to ventilate and some to drain the mines, were dug. This resulted in many tons of unprofitable stone, which was strewn across the fellsides. Miners used the levels for easy access to the face and worked eight-hour shifts. This gave time for the harmful dust to settle.

The industry reached its peak during the eighteenth and nineteenth centuries when worked by the Quaker London Lead Company who rented the land from the Greenwich Hospital. They genuinely tried to improve the life of the miner and helped them to build small-holdings on hillsides near to the mines. They subsidized libraries, schools and the construction of good roads.

It was still a very hard life, however, and, in the eighteenth century a miner could only expect to live to about thirty-five years of age. In 1842, figures produced showed that 88 out of Alston's 100 widows receiving Parish Relief had been lead miners' wives. After a General Board of Health Inspection in 1858 it was found that Alston had a higher proportion of widows than any other place in Britain and there was not a single miner whose sputum was not stained by the blue-black dust ingested during the working day. By this time the life expectancy had increased by another ten years.

In 1882, the company sold their leases to the Nenthead and Tynehead Lead and Zinc company for £30,000 and by the end of the century mining on a large scale ceased. Most miners abandoned their uneconomic small-holdings, which were left to decay along with the mine-workings.

Relaxing in Garrigill.

landmark in the walk for we have now conquered the toughest section. The green valley is an oasis amongst desolate moorland from which the official Pennine Way now spares us - from here to the Wall we follow riverbanks and valleys!

Garrigill, which means Gerrard's Valley, lies in seclusion by the banks of the South Tyne, well away from the main Middleton to Alston road. This pleasant village has a large green, lined by old stone dwellings. Its development probably stemmed from its nearness to the lead mines on Cross Fell. The George and Dragon is a fine inn. Having often stayed there, I can thoroughly recommend the food and hospitality. Try their sticky toffee pudding - it's just what the doctor ordered!

THE SOUTH TYNE VALLEY

Travellers from Dufton will be weary by now and may choose to stop at Garrigill. Those who are Alston-bound continue on the west side of the South Tyne until a footbridge at GR 724429 is used to cross to the opposite tree-lined banks close to Sillyhall Farm. Here the path veers away from the river, climbing across high pastures to Bleagate Farm. A succession of fields are traversed above the South Tyne, which flows over a wide stony bed. Views are restricted by concave eastern slopes and dominated by the high wild moors to the west but the impetus of pressing on to Alston probably keeps most eyes and minds directly ahead.

ALSTON

The path becomes a well-defined walled track for the last mile and meets the A686 road at the majestic twin-arched stone bridge over the river. From here it is a short but uphill walk to Alston's centre. The village is isolated from the rest of England and it certainly feels that way, surrounded by high fells on all sides. The isolation was increased when the railway line to Haltwhistle was closed in the seventies. Being around a thousand feet above sea level, it is often snowed-in during winter months.

Among the cobbled streets and stone buildings is a fine market cross and the square-towered church with a high, pointed spire stands proud from the rooftops behind the main street. John Wesley came to preach here in 1748.

Facilities for the Pennine Way walker include many inns, a camp-site and a youth hostel. This is also a good place to restock supplies.

The market place, Alston.

NOTE ON ALTERNATIVE ROUTES

There are few alternatives to the High Pennine section. Almost all walkers will want to climb to Cross Fell, unless weather conditions are poor. The area is part of a Nature Reserve run by the Nature Conservancy Council who seem very opposed to any activities (including walking) except their own. As such, there is no free access.

One possibility during foul weather, although still inferior to the official line, is to straddle the fells via Dufton's neighbouring village of Knock, reached by country lane. As the lane through the village turns sharp left (GR 682269) take the track leading north-eastwards, skirting the eastern side of Knock Pike. The track becomes a path beyond the Pike and continues about 50 yards to the west of Swindale Beck, passing through gates and a stile *en route* to meeting the metalled radar station lane half-way up Knock Fell. The lane climbs steeply to attain the ridge to the south-east of the station and continues northwards sharing the line with the official Pennine Way.

As the metalled track veers left (GR 717317) you take a less prominent track, which descends north-wards at first, then eastwards, parallel to the line of Dunfell Hush (not marked on 1:50000 maps). The track degenerates into a path and heads for Trout Beck, whose northern banks are traced. Shortly before the confluence with the infant Tees, a wide track from

Moor House, a former shooting hut now owned by the Nature Conservancy Council, is joined. This continues by the banks of Trout Beck and crosses the Tees via a bridge close to the old Teesdale Mine. Beyond the bridge the stony track doubles back westwards to climb the wild moorland expanses between Tyne Head Fell and Round Hill before dropping into the valley of the South Tyne. Beyond the farm of Dorthgill the old miners' track becomes a country lane that rejoins the Pennine Way at Garrigill, 2 miles distant.

ROUTE FILE	
Maps	OS.Landranger (1:50000) Nos 91 'Appleby-in-Westmorland' and 86 'Haltwhistle & Alston': Outdoor Leisure Map (1:25000) No. 31 'Teesdale' would be useful.
Distance and time Official Way	19 miles (30km) 12 hours
Terrain	Stiff climb to Knock Fell then good ridge paths to Cross Fell (with the exception of marshy ground at Tees Head). It descends to Garrigill on good stony tracks and continues on riverside paths from Garrigill to Alston.
Accommodation	B&Bs and an inn at Garrigill; youth hostel, inns, B&Bs and a camp-site at Alston.
Shops	At Garrigill and Alston.
Tourist Information	Robinson's School, Middlegate, Penrith, Cumbria, CA11 7PT. Tel. 0768 67466.

12

THROUGH GLENS AND DALES TO THE ROMAN WALL
Alston to Hadrian's Wall

For this section, the official route leaves the high hills and continues along the valley of the South Tyne. The loftiest fells lie to the west but these are grouse moors and no rights of way traverse their tops.

The itinerary is, at times, complex and route-finding among fields and farmyards can be distracting. Never far away are the Maiden Way (an old Roman road), the river, the Brampton Road or the disused railway that once linked Alston with Haltwhistle.

It is mostly a very pleasant walk that complements the high ridges of Cross Fell but in the latter stages there are dull uninteresting stretches of derelict marshy moor and pastureland punctuated by unsightly opencast mines and quarries. But always those high fells to

the west tower mockingly above. In the distance, however, the Whin Sill crags close to Hadrian's Wall promise better things to come.

For my alternative route I chose a climb over Hard Rigg and Mohope Moor to the West Allen, a valley as beautiful as any Yorkshire Dale. The walk, which continues over high pastures through woodland and by riverbanks is memorable and far superior to the official way!

Both routes lead to Hadrian's Wall, but some ten miles apart. The official route joins at Thirlwall Castle, near Greenhead and my alternative at Winshield Crags, north-west of Bardon Mill. Both are well served by accommodation.

Opposite page: The South Tyne at Garrigill.   *Below: On the Mohope Moor track above Blagill looking back towards Alston.*

ALSTON TO GREENHEAD
The Official Route

ALSTON

On the official Pennine Way we have to say goodbye to high fells until the Cheviots of Northumbria. Tom Stephenson must have looked long and hard at those hills to the west for surely a purist Pennine route would go the length of them, probably dropping down to the valley at Brampton from Cold Fell. He would, I suspect, have been thwarted by the interests of the grouse-shooting fraternity. The route he did choose keeps to the western side of the valley, sometimes across farmland and sometimes on the shoulders of the moor.

From Alston Bridge, the way follows a northbound track along the South Tyne's western banks behind some charming renovated stone cottages. Beyond the cottages, it becomes a grassy groove in lush fields and gives good views of Alston, which occupies an elevated position across the river.

After passing through some decorative gates, we are confronted by Harbut Lodge, a beautiful old mansion that was sadly damaged by fire. The fine sandstone building is kept to the right and, after circumventing the coach-house, the path traces the edge of a field before joining a tree-lined drive, which meets the A689 Brampton Road at GR 708474. A path to the north of Harbut Law Farm opposite (not named on OS maps) climbs westwards across fields to a stile by a wall corner (GR 703474). The OS maps suggest a detour

On the village green at Slaggyford.

around the woods on Wanwood Hill but the way everybody now uses is marked by the stile. A well-defined path that has become a green ribbon on the rough moorland descends north-westwards to the depression cut by Gilderdale Burn, which is crossed via a metal footbridge.

WHITLEY CASTLE

The path then arcs around the old Roman fort of Whitley Castle, built to guard the Maiden Way, one of the great supply roads to the frontier at Carvoran near Thirlwall Castle on Hadrian's Wall. The six rings of ditches are very pronounced and are possibly the best preserved in Britain.

The A689 is again crossed after passing through the farmyard of Castle Nook. The route continues north adjacent to the line of the Maiden Way and close to the disused railway line. By Lintley Farm it goes under a railway viaduct and then follows the course, firstly of Thornhope Burn then of the South Tyne, which now flows on a wide stony bed with trees lining its banks.

SLAGGYFORD

The main road, encountered once more at GR 681519, is then followed to the sleepy village of

Crossing Glendue Burn.

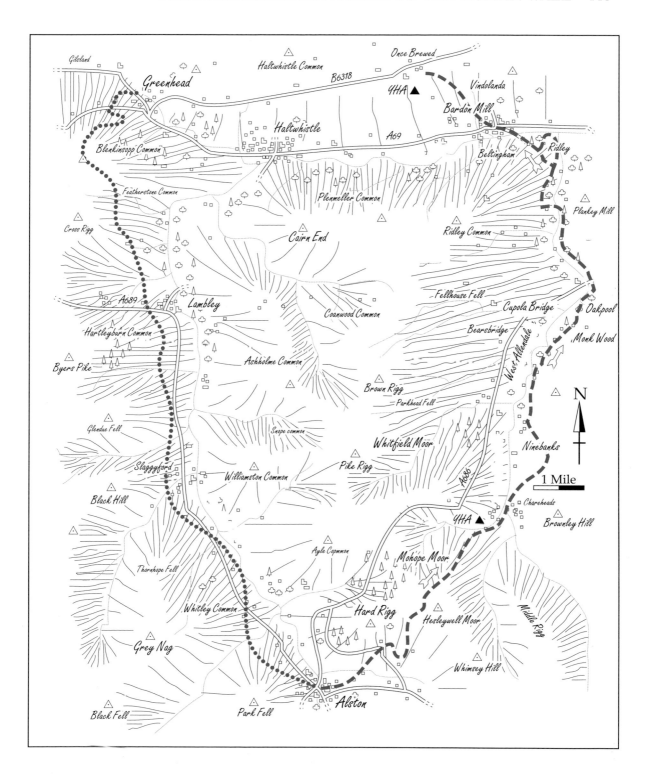

Heading across the wastelands near Lambley Colliery.

Slaggyford. Here terraced cottages line a wide village green and the grassy slopes of Williamston Common rise high to the east. A track by the chapel to the west of the village leads north-westwards by the old railway line before dropping into a sheltered glade beneath a stone-built railway viaduct. At the foot of the viaduct a small footbridge crosses Knar Burn before climbing its opposite banks. It passes under the railway at another small bridge to the north. A track then leads across fields past Merry Knowe Farm to another viaduct at the farming hamlet of Burnstones by the main road. Close by at the hamlet of Knarsdale is the Kirkstyle Inn, which offers refreshments and food to the hungry traveller.

Beyond Burnstones the Pennine Way again follows the Maiden Way, traversing the lower slopes of Glendue Fell. We have now left the farmlands behind and embark upon simpler moorland routes. After descending to cross the picturesque Glendue Burn, the route continues northwards to the left of a wall, traversing more marshy, heather-clad moors. Views across the Tyne-Solway Gap to the Whin Sill crags in the region of the Wall are opening up, giving a hint of better things to come. Unfortunately there are still a few miles of dreary countryside to be covered.

The fence is crossed at a stile and recrossed at another. The second stile marks the divergence from the Maiden Way on a vague path meeting the A689 Brampton road at GR 663586. On the opposite side of the road the route continues northwards past the disused Lambley Colliery, which is set among infertile, unkempt and marshy pastures. The wall that guides the path veers right at GR 663590 by Black Burn. The route maintains this direction, making first for a tall post lying on a firm island within a boggy reed-covered expanse and then for a gate leading to yet more boggy wastelands.

HARTLEY BURN

The path descends to cross a streamlet before climbing its opposite banks to reach the ruin of High House. This is perched above the much more verdant scenery surrounding Hartley Burn, a meandering tree-lined watercourse. A winding narrow track descends on steep wooded slopes to a footbridge spanning the burn. Beyond it the route follows the eastern banks until the watercourse bends to the left. The path then climbs out of the depression, veers left high above Hartley Burn, and continues north-westwards to Ulpham and Batey Shield Farms.

FEATHERSTONE COMMON

After crossing the minor road to the north of Batey Shield Farm, the path continues past the cottage of

Greenriggs (at GR 654613, unnamed on 1:50000 maps). Beyond is Featherstone Common, which must be crossed on a north-west traverse of its vast, uninviting moors. It is easy to go wrong in the area around Glencune Burn and it is better to take compass bearings than to follow misleading sheep-tracks.

After crossing the burn, the path comes to a stile close to the intersection of a ridge fence and stone wall. The stile is scaled and the ridge fence followed, passing the ruins of Eadleystone. When the fence deviates to the west, head towards the summit trig. point of Wain Rigg, which lies beyond a dry-stone wall. A path then descends to a barn beneath a line of electricity pylons. It continues northwards to an old chalet where a right turn is made along a track passing the awful scars created by opencast coal mines and quarries. After circumventing these works, a cart track leads northwards to the busy A69 Newcastle to Carlisle road. This is crossed before climbing the banks on its opposite side and crossing the fields by a golf course.

GREENHEAD

At GR 653658 we turn right, tracing the course of the Vallum, a great ditch dug by the Romans along the length of Hadrian's Wall. This leads eastwards to the road north of Greenhead village and directly opposite Thirlwall Castle, which is perched on a bank above a cluster of charming cottages.

There is a youth hostel and inn at Greenhead, and it is a natural place to break the walk. Tomorrow should be a better day, for the trek along the wall is uncomplicated and, in places, spectacular. We will walk through history.

ALSTON TO THE WALL
An Alternative Route via West Allendale

This alternative route tackles Mohope Moor before dropping into the valley of the West Allen, where memories of the Yorkshire Dales come flooding back.

ALSTON

A little ginnel to the east of the market cross leads past tightly enclosed cottages to a cart track following the southern banks of the swift-flowing River Nent.

Traces of the underlying coal face are found on the surface of the track. A fine stone bridge (GR 725468) by some waterfalls is crossed and the succeeding path

Thirlwall Castle.

rakes up verdant hill pastures away from the river and towards Corby Gates Farm. Retrospective views of Alston are impressive and include the High Pennines on the skyline.

BLAGILL AND MOHOPE MOOR

Beyond the farm, after crossing two stiles in high stone walls, the path continues by another wall (on the left) to the road at Blagill (GR 739474). The place is very aptly named for here coal is never very far below the surface and private collieries proliferate.

The lane meets the B6294 road, which is then used to circumvent Blagill Burn. At GR 741475, an old mine road is followed eastwards for a mile where it joins another track north of West Cocklake Farm. Here we climb on the northbound walled track to the high moors east of the trig. point at Hard Rigg. It terminates at the ridge and a rutted moorland track continues before being abandoned for an old route known as Carriers Way. The terrain is virtually trackless and, as such, compass readings should be used. Keep to the west of Mohope Burn's hollow and aim for Mohope Head. Here we get a first glimpse of the beautiful valley of the West Allen, where woods and lush fields are capped by pale high moors.

From Mohope Head a cart track leads safely down the fell to reach a narrow metalled lane at Fairplay Farm. This passes a youth hostel, Orchard House.

WEST ALLENDALE

The lane descends among farm pastures on a spur between the Whitewalls and Wellhope Burns, both

Above: The West Allen Valley near Ninebanks. Right: In the Allen Gorge north of Cupola Bridge.

tributaries of the West Allen. It reaches the West Allen by a stone bridge, tucked away in a quiet corner beneath tall, tree-fringed banks. Perched high above, partially obscured by the trees, is a small church with an impressive spire. After crossing the West Allen via the stone bridge, steps from the right hand side of the road climb the banks to the higher Ninebanks lane and the church.

DRYBURN CLOUGH

There is now a delightful series of footpaths which climb the hillsides to the east, encircling Dryburn Clough. The walk around this area is fascinating, although complex in places (it would be a good idea to have the Pathfinder map NY65/75 (Slaggyford) for route-finding).

To the left of the church, a footpath climbs north-eastwards on the steep, trackless slopes of a field, passing to the left of some trees on the horizon. The route continues across the field, going through a wide opening in the wall close to its left hand corner. After following the wall on the left, go through the first gate beyond a junction of walls. An east-north-easterly direction across the next field will then lead to a barn before continuing on a cart track to the old farm of Far Dryburn (GR 792532).

Beyond Far Dryburn, the path descends by a wall into Dryburn Clough. A quaint stone pack-horse bridge at the edge of mixed woodland is used to cross the stream. This small but lively watercourse drains Dryburn Moor, whose barren slopes can be seen in contrasting sullen scenes beyond Dryburn Hall.

After crossing a stile by the bridge, the path leads northwards across fields to Birk Hott Farm (GR 794536). A short cart track then leads to the derelict farm buildings of Birken before crossing more fields to the larger Mount Pleasant Farm. From here a track leads to the country lane linking Ninebanks with Allendale Town.

MONK WOOD

Although a path is shown on the opposite side of the road it has been blocked in two places. A simpler way is to turn right along the lane then left at the next junction. A track from GR 791549 then descends westwards, passing between Low House and Gate House Farms. Beyond the farms it veers northwards on a course parallel to the West Allen, which meanders below. It is very easy to go wrong at the apex of the bend and follow a prominent lower track by a row of trees. This will lead down to a riverside camping and

caravan site. The correct track, which deviates by a large tree, is much higher and climbs gradually to meet and follow a dry-stone wall at the top of the field to a gate marking the entrance to Monk Wood.

The wide track through Monk Wood is easy to walk and the environment is lovely - the trees are a pleasant mix of conifer and deciduous. Bluebells and rhododendrons clothe the floor, adding vivid splashes of colour in spring and early summer. Through the trees, on the far banks of the West Allen, the magnificent mansion of Whitfield Hall can be seen, set among emerald lawns.

Monk Farm lies at the northern edge of the woods. A gate on its northern side precedes a climb to Harlow Bower Farm. If the lower (western) edge of the field is followed to a gate, a yellow arrow then points the way uphill to a telegraph post. A line of these posts then leads to a stile at the top edge of the field. After a short climb north-eastwards to Harlow Bower, a cart track provides access to a country lane at GR 795571.

EAST ALLENDALE

We now descend into the valley of the East Allen. The lane is followed for a couple of hundred yards eastwards before turning left on the very narrow Oakpool Lane, which crosses the River East Allen before climbing the pastures of Old Town. Views across the top of the sylvan Allen Gorge to the craggy outlines of Hadrian's Wall country are wide and impressive, but the best of the day is yet to come!

A left turn at the junction (GR 817587) then leads past High Staward to the A686, half a mile to the north-east of Cupola Bridge. The path shown as descending the gorge from immediately opposite the road is non-existent. Forty yards eastwards, along the busy road, a farm track descends across fields to the ruins of Gingle Pot Farm.

THE ALLEN GORGE

A faint path, shown by black dotted lines on the 1:50000 OS maps, then descends north-westwards to the edge of the woodlands of the Allen Gorge, which are entered via a small gate (GR 804605). The track through these delightful mixed woodlands is well defined and a pleasure to walk. In the early stages we are high on the glen's eastern flanks high above the lively river, which can be glimpsed through the trees. There is a junction of paths by two huge stone gateposts. Although both routes are acceptable, the one to the right, which follows a stone wall, is more clear. It is bordered by profuse banks of wild garlic and blue-bell, emitting a rich aroma during the spring and summer months.

At Hag Bank the path comes close to the river, whose lively course is channelled by steep cliffs and gigantic slabs rising from its rocky bed. There are many marvellous spots in this vicinity for a lunch or tea break.

ALLEN BANKS

The path temporarily leaves the woods and crosses a field by the riverbanks to Plankey Mill, where there is an excellent camp-site. (They also sell ice creams and minerals) The River Allen is crossed here and another bridge straddles a tributary, Kingswood Beck, before well-used woodland paths continue northwards. One route is high level and the other by the riverside - take your pick. These are the Allen Banks Plantations and are owned by the National Trust, whose car park, picnic site and collection box are at the northern end by Ridley College.

BARDON MILL

After leaving Allen Banks, a tree-lined country lane is followed westwards through the hamlet of Beltingham. Here we reacquaint ourselves with the South Tyne (not seen since Alston). It is crossed using the footbridge at GR 782643 and a track continues northwards over the Newcastle to Carlisle railway line to reach the village of Bardon Mill. There is an inn for those who want to stop the night here but those who wish to carry on can

continue along the lane opposite, signposted to Thorngrafton. This goes northwards under the main A69 road.

VINDOLANDA

Left turns are taken at the next two junctions, followed by a right. At GR 772653 the lanes are abandoned for a picturesque route heading for the Wall country. The path traverses a field to reach the edge of a wooded glen. It then traces the edge northwards, passing a whitewashed cottage before descending over lush meadows towards the stream. In views to the left a reconstructed Roman fort, Vindolanda, can be seen on high grassy banks. The fort was first constructed in AD90 and is part of a vast Roman complex that has been extensively excavated.

Further north, after crossing the stream via a small footbridge, the path passes through the ornamental grounds of the Vindolanda Trust's museum and café.

ONCE BREWED, HADRIAN'S WALL

Country lanes then lead to the youth hostel and Information Centre at Once Brewed (Twice Brewed on 1:50000 maps). Camping is available at Winshields Farm and there are a few hotels in Haltwhistle, 5 miles to the west.

ROUTE FILE	
Maps	OS Landranger (1:50000) No. 86 'Haltwhistle & Alston'
Distance and time Official Way Alternative via Allendale	16 miles (26km) 9 hours 21 miles (33km) 12 hours
Terrain	Very little ascent on official way. Paths on low moors. The alternative route traverses Mohope Moor where the paths are very faint. This is followed by some riverside walking and paths over lofty farmland.
Accommodation	B&Bs at Slaggyford; inn at Knarsdale; youth hostel and B&Bs at Greenhead. On the alternative route there is a youth hostel and B&B at Ninebanks; an inn and B&B at Bardon Mill and an inn and youth hostel at Once Brewed.
Shops	Greenhead. At Plankey Mill and Bardon Mill on the alternative route.
Tourist Information	The Manor Office, Hallgate, Hexham, Northumberland. NE46 1XD tel. 00434 605225.

13

THE ROMAN WALL AND THE GREAT FORESTS

Hadrian's Wall to Kielder/Bellingham

The Pennine Way traces the finest section of Hadrian's Wall between Thirlwall and Rapishaw Gap. Here the undulating Whin Sill ridge offers superb walking with the added attractions of Roman relics. We are walking along with ancient history firing the imagination.

The crag-studded moorland to be traversed immediately north of the wall can appear desolate but the sun can transform the scenes into dramatic weather-beaten landscapes with a glint of gold.

The official and alternative routes part company near Stonehaugh on the eastern edge of the great Border Forests. The official route continues through forest rides and low moors before descending into Bellingham, a small but lively market town on the banks of the North Tyne.

My alternative route unashamedly follows flinted forestry roads through the vast plantations of Wark and Kielder to surface at the large reservoir of Kielder Water. The reward for using this route will be reaped on the next day when the relatively featureless moors north of Bellingham are traded for the wild hillscapes of Kielder Head.

Looking east along the course of Hadrian's Wall from from Winshields Crag, showing Highshield Crag and Crag Lough (lake).

THIRLWALL CASTLE
TO BELLINGHAM
The Official Route

THIRLWALL CASTLE

A gate from the B6318 Gilsland Road marks the start of a track, which passes a terrace of red-bricked houses before crossing the railway line (take care). The route then traces the edge of a field adjacent to a small stream before passing through a tiny hamlet dominated by the ruins of Thirlwall Castle, which is perched on a small hillock. The castle was built approximately 700 years ago from stone robbed from Hadrian's Wall. Edward I is said to have stopped here in 1306 while fighting the Scots.

The way crosses the burn on the footbridge in the centre of the hamlet and continues on a zig-zag walled track to some woods before striking out eastwards along the line of a ditch that had been built on the northern side of Hadrian's Wall (stones hereabouts were robbed for the castle). A narrow lane is reached on the far side of the pastures. After going southwards

Hadrian's Wall near Walltown Crags.

for a hundred yards along it, a Pennine Way signpost points the way to Walltown Quarry, which has recently been landscaped to hide the scars of past industry.

A stony side road then leads eastwards but it is soon abandoned for a route heading uphill for the Wall itself. This it meets close to Turret 45a. The Wall is nowhere near complete but is none the less thrilling to see. It is easy to imagine the magnificent original construction straddling the undulating crests - dominant and, to the enemy, foreboding.

WALLTOWN CRAGS

The official line of the Pennine Way follows the course of an old Roman military way but most people keep to the crest of the ridge by the course of the Wall. Walltown Crags are sheer but softened in places by rowan and ash trees that have grown in the more sheltered spots. The wall itself has disappeared hereabouts and has been replaced with a more modest dry-stone farm wall. Turret 44b is passed beyond a small dip close to Walltown Farm and the way climbs to the wind-blown craggy heights of Cockmount Hill. Ahead are superb, spacious panoramas encompassing

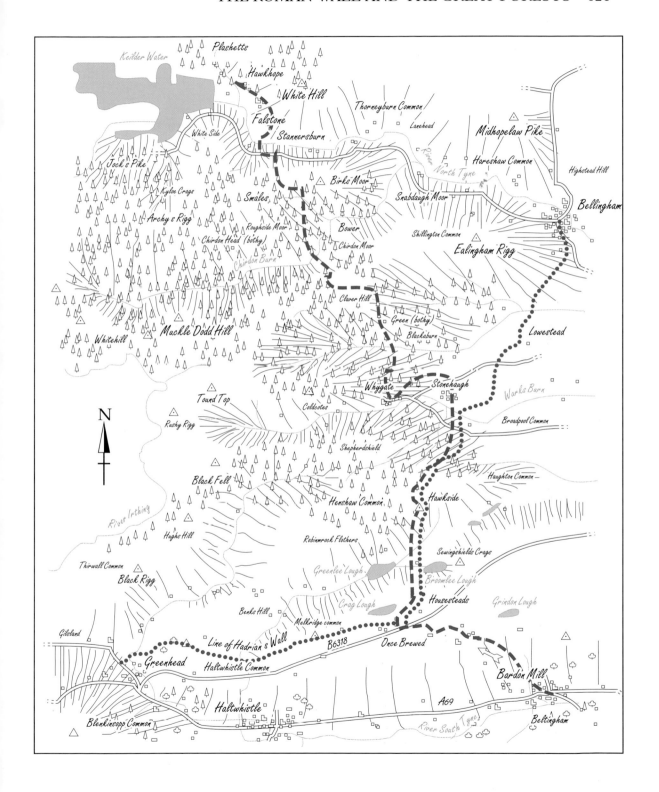

Climbers on Peel Crags above Crag Lough (lake).

Winshields Crag, Steel Rigg and Sewingshields Crag. To the north is the expansive blue-green mantle of the Kielder Forest extending to the horizon while to the south are the bright green fields of the South Tyne Valley.

On descending to the pastures of Cockmount Hill Farm, some unsignposted earthworks will be noticed.

Rapishaw Gap where the wall is abandoned for the trek north.

These are the remains of Great Chesters Fort. From here an obvious course guided by a dry-stone wall leads to the road opposite Cawfields Quarry.

CAWFIELDS

A cart track from the road leads past the old quarry and picnic site. The quarrying activities have destroyed the Wall and the artificial lake formed from the excavations does little to enhance the scene. One cannot wait to leave it behind. Normality is resumed on the ridge of Cawfield Crags. Milecastle 42 is well preserved and the Wall well restored. The views are once more wide-sweeping and unblemished. Trees and shrubs have strangely thrived among the crags, tenuously clinging to exposed grassy ledges and steely screes.

WINSHIELDS CRAG

After descending briefly to the minor road-crossing at Caw Gap, the path climbs to Winshields Crag, which, at 1230 ft (448m), is the highest point on the wall. From this fine viewpoint we can look back and see the High Pennines including Cross Fell, the northern Lake

North of the wall near Greenlee Lough looking towards King's Crag.

District Peaks and the Solway Firth. Ahead, in the middle distance, are the crags of Steel Rigg and Hotbanks, with the fine lake, Crag Lough, sandwiched between.

A descent is made to another road straddling the ridge. Beyond a roadside National Trust car park our route along the wall continues. After a short way it veers right to descend to a grassy depression beneath the impressive buttresses of Peel Crag, most popular with climbers. A steep climb, aided by steps, follows to the ridge of Steel Rigg. The wall here is wider and taller than has been seen previously and Milecastle 39 is the best preserved on the entire route. It is easy to imagine the Roman soldiers patrolling the harsh outposts of their huge empire.

Beyond Steel Rigg we pass above Crag Lough, a grand lake, huddled beneath the screes and dark cliffs of Highshield Crag, also popular with climbers. Notable are the dolerite pinnacles, which are supposedly easy to climb. After descending north-westwards to Hotbank Farm, the route climbs to Hotbank Crags. Here the pleasant Broomlee Lough comes into view beneath shapely Sewingshields Crags.

RAPISHAW GAP
At Rapishaw Gap (GR 781687, and not named on 1:50000 maps) the Pennine Way and my alternative route abandon the line of the wall although a detour could be made to see the extensive remains of Housesteads Fort, which lie just to the east (entrance fees are paid at the adjacent museum).

The Pennine Way heads north-north-east over moorland to the west of Broomlee Lough. Ahead are the plantations of the Wark Forest, outliers of the massive Border Forest Park. After descending to cross Jenkins Burn the undulating track regains height to Crag End, where Greenlee Lough comes into view. The lake lies beneath dark north-facing crags where a lonely tree warped by the elements adds drama to the surroundings. In the opposite direction is a complex landscape of ridges and crags - the most notable being the weird-shaped Kings Crag.

A wide, grassy path descends from Crag End towards the lake before doubling back and resuming its course towards the forest.

WARK FOREST TO STONEHAUGH
The forest is encountered at GR 780708, close to East Stonefolds Farm and the way continues on flinted roads until GR 782718, where a grassy ride is followed to the plantation's north-eastern edge. The moors of Haughton Common are bare and rolling. The Knoll of Hawkside is kept to the right and the path heads east-

A HISTORY OF HADRIAN'S WALL

In AD43 the Roman Emperor Claudius decided to enhance his reputation by extending the Empire northwards to Britain. His armies, led by Agricola, duly crossed the sea and easily overran the southern counties but found the northern barbarians more resilient. They set up a temporary frontier (the Stangate) between the Tyne Valley and the Solway Firth before venturing further to conquer lands between the Forth and Clyde.

In AD85 Agricola was recalled and the troops retreated to the Tyne-Solway Gap. After a visit in AD122, Emperor Hadrian decided to build his now famous wall. It was originally planned to span 76 miles between the River Irthing at Thirlwall and Newcastle. In addition a turf wall would extend to Bowness on Solway.

The main wall was to be 15ft high and 10ft wide (Later sections were reduced in size in order to speed up the construction). On the northern side a V-shaped ditch, 30ft wide and 10ft deep, was excavated, except where crags made this unnecessary. Fortified gateways (milecastles) were built along the length of the wall at one mile intervals in order to allow passage for through traffic and access to the wall top. They would also each act as a barracks for eight soldiers. Between the milecastles, at intervals of one third of a mile, were turrets, which served as observation posts.

Additions and modifications were made. It was decided to extend the wall from Newcastle to Wallsend and a few towers were constructed along the Cumbrian Coast. Large forts were built close to the wall if geographical conditions would allow. Great Chesters, Carrawbergh, Carvoran and Housesteads numbered among these, while Birdoswald stood by the turf wall. A second ditch, the Vallum was dug on the south side of the wall thus enclosing their military area.

After Hadrian's death, Agricola's Forth–Clyde line was re-established and the Antonine Wall was constructed. Hadrian's Wall was opened to let traffic through. In AD200, however , the Romans were forced to withdraw to their former positions and Hadrian's Wall was repaired.

After the Roman withdrawal from Britain, successive centuries saw the gradual destruction of the wall, whose stone was robbed for the building of churches, farmhouses and field walls. After the 1745 rebellion a military road was built using, for many miles, the Roman Wall as foundations.

The twentieth century has seen Hadrian's Wall lovingly restored and it is not difficult to imagine the desolate times of the red-cloaked centurions patrolling the high parapets.

Turret in the wall at Cawfields.

Houxty Burn.

north-east for a small cluster of Scots pine on the horizon. After passing an enclosed tarn, more plantations are entered via a ladder stile. From here, further forest rides lead to a country lane near Willowbog Farm. Turn right along the lane, which climbs to Ladyhill before being abandoned for a grassy forest track. This leads to yet another narrow tarmac lane at GR 803754 where the official route and my alternative part company. The former continues over forest, moor and farm pasture to the village of Bellingham, while the latter goes deep into the forest to Kielder Water.

On the official route we are released from the confines of the forest for a fair distance on Broadpool Common. A signpost at the plantation's edge points the way across the moor. The sketchy track follows closely the banks of a stream in the middle stages, passing a small waterfall before fording Fawlee Syke.

WARKS BURN
On climbing the opposite bank to a ladder stile, pleasant scenes are revealed across the sylvan dene of Warks Burn to the pale heather-clad hillsto the north of Bellingham. From the stile the route descends by a line of twisted hawthorn trees towards Warks Burn, which it crosses by means of a steel footbridge. The path continues to the farm of Horneystead where B&B and teas are available, thence to a minor road via The Ash (farm). Immediately opposite, by Leadgate Farm, a signposted path leads past some small crags down to the superbly renovated bastle (fortified farmhouse) of Low Stead, sheltered by trees in the dip of Blacka Burn.

After passing through the farmyard a track leads northwards and then veers to the east on a metalled lane to a junction. It then turns left (north-north-east) along a metalled lane to another junction (GR 826793). This time road walking is abandoned and the same direction is maintained across a field, accompanied by a fence and wind-warped hawthorns. A descent is then made towards Houxty Burn. The hillside pastures beyond the meandering tree-lined stream are highlighted by small copses and farmsteads, and

Above: Bellingham from the lane at the foot of Ealingham Rigg.   *Opposite: Smales Farm near Kielder Water.*

higher up they are fringed by a narrow band of rocks known as Shitlington Crags.

SHITLINGTON CRAGS

After crossing Houxty Burn on the small footbridge the path turns right following the banks to a signposted cart track leading past Shitlington Hall, which is in fact a plain farmhouse. The route climbs north-westwards then northwards across fields before passing behind a more austere dwelling, Shitlington Crag Farm. A track now threads through the spartan sandstone crags to traverse the grassy moors beyond. On the crest of the hill, close to a radio mast, an old track by a wall is followed eastwards skirting the heather moors of Ealingham Rigg. After a third of a mile, a Pennine Way sign points the way north-eastwards across rough pastures.

BELLINGHAM

The busy little market town of Bellingham lies snugly in the green valley of the North Tyne beneath the heather moors that rise to Padon Hill. In late summer the moors glow with the purple flame of a myriad blooms. A minor road is encountered at GR 841817 and this is followed briefly before crossing fields to the left and meeting the B6320 a mile short of Bellingham Village. The road is conveyed across the wide North Tyne River on a fine three-arched stone bridge, which was built in the 1830s. It continues uphill and then into the pleasant town where the shops can supply most of the supplies needed to finish this long walk.

STONEHAUGH TO KIELDER
An Alternative Route

After beginning deliciously over the undulating ridges of Hadrian's Wall this route continues in relatively dull fashion through forests of larch and spruce. Thankfully, a good pace can be made on wide flinted forestry tracks and the way may be enlivened by the sighting of a sparrowhawk soaring in the skies in search of prey. Red squirrel and roe deer are also residents of the area. The latter are more likely to be 'out of cover' early morning or in the evening.

STONEHAUGH

The country lane is followed from GR 803754 north of Ladyhill Farm through the hamlet of Stonehaugh to a T-junction south of Birk Hill. This lane is followed westwards toWhygate Farm where a right turn is taken. A left turn along a track at GR 773761 then leads north-westwards across open land before entering Wark Forest to the east of Harelaw.

CHIRDON BURN

Continuing north-westwards on a wide forestry road, the Clinton Burn is crossed at a place strangely known

as Irish Bridge and Chirdon Burn, west of the Chirdon Head (a bothie). The flinted track ends at Shepherd's Burn (GR 724829). The grassy track to be followed now has a fire tower on its left hand side. At the time of writing, the path at its termination has been obscured by the felling of mature trees beyond GR 722837 but I am promised by the Forestry Commission that they will waymark and reinstate it to the edge of the plantation.

SMALES

It is good to be in the open again and there are wide views over the valley of the North Tyne to the Cheviot Hills. The path (trackless) continues northwards until reaching a fence, which is then followed down to Smales Farm.

After turning right at the farmhouse, the path leads northwards, passing through a gate at the next field boundary before reaching a complex network of Forestry Roads. It is possible to continue along the bridleway but much easier and quicker to turn left along the forestry road then double-back (right) on another road, which descends to Stannersburn. Here the local inn offers a fine standard of food and accommodation.

FALSTONE

There is a shop and more accommodation at Falstone village, which lies beneath the huge Kielder Dam. The Blackcock Inn is very popular. Camp-sites are located on the shores of Kielder Water at Leaplish and also at Kielder village but it may be better to check the list of forestry back-packing sites in the route file (no facilities are offered but no charges are made at present).

ROUTE FILE

Maps	OS Landranger (1:50000) Nos 86 'Haltwhistle & Alston' and 80 'The Cheviot'
Distance and time	
Official Way	21 miles (33km) 12 hours
Alternative to Kielder	17 miles (27km) 13 hours
Terrain	Good ridge paths Hadrian's Wall, followed by forest paths and tracks on both routes.
Accommodation	Camp-site and B&B at Winshields; camp-site at Stonehaugh; inns, B&Bs, a youth hostel and camp-site at Bellingham. On the alternative route there are backpacking camp-sites in the Kielder Forest (see below); bothies run by the Mountain Bothies Association in the Kielder Forest at Green (GR 740786) and Chirdon Head (GR 719812); inns at Stannersburn and Falstone; camp-sites with full facilities at Leaplish and Kielder. The Forestry Enterprise (formerly the Forestry Commission) kindly offer a number of free backpacking campsites (no facilities) within the Kielder Forest. They must be booked at least 3 days in advance and they need to know your route through the forest. They, in turn, will advise you of any problems that might arise or detours which may be necessary. Write to Kielder Forest District Office, Forestry Enterprise, Eels Burn, Bellingham, Hexham, Northumberland. The sites are at Allery Bank (GR 748814); The D Field, Smales Burn (GR 721850); Belling (GR 691899) and Plashetts (GR 662902).
Shops	At Stonehaugh and Bellingham. At Falstone and Kielder on the alternative route.
Tourist Information	The Manor Office, Hallgate, Hexham, Northumberland. NE46 1XD. Tel. 00434 605225 or for Kielder alternative route -Tower Knowe, Kielder Water, Northumberland, NE48 1BY. TEL 0434 240398.

Kielder Water at sunset and in the early morning mists.

14

THROUGH THE LANDS OF THE BORDER REIVERS

Bellingham/Kielder to Byrness

The two routes offered on this penultimate section are completely different. The official route picks its way across farmland, over the heather moors of Padon Hill and through the great Border Forest plantations before reaching Byrness in the Redesdale Valley. The route has its highlights, such as the valley of Warks Burn and the view from Padon Hill, but it is little more than a preamble for the last day on the High Cheviots.

In contrast, the alternative route, which begins at Falstone by Kielder Water, introduces us to the Cheviot Hills a day earlier. Although not as high as those encountered on the last stage, the heather-clad, craggy hills on the Kielder side of Carter Bar are wilder, feel more remote and are every bit as dramatic.

The approach along the valley of the White Kielder Burn invites us into tranquil and seldom visited countryside. It is a haven for wildlife, including roe deer, feral goats and birds of prey. From the high moors there is a bird's eye view of the main Cheviot ridge before the final descent into Byrness.

The lonely moors at Kielder Head seen on the alternative route.

BELLINGHAM TO BYRNESS
The Official Route

BELLINGHAM

From the village centre the West Woodburn road is taken, crossing the bridge over Hareshaw Burn. The winding lane then climbs past the youth hostel. It is abandoned at the sharp, right-hand bend (GR 846837) for a track heading northwards to Blakelaw Farm. After passing through the farmyard on to hillside pastureland to its north-west, the way climbs north-westwards to a marker post. A faint path leads to a wall corner and then onwards to a gate in a dry stone wall to the east of a small pine plantation.

The prominent track traverses moorland, which is clad with mat grass and heather and fringed with the dark rocks of Callerhues Crag. To the west the hill slopes decline to the tree-enshrouded defile of Hareshaw Burn.

The current OS maps show the Pennine Way climbing the moorland to the west of the crag and entering the farmyard of Hareshaw House. This would involve taking a right fork in the moorland tracks east of the Hareshaw Linn Falls. However, a preferred alternative takes the left fork and keeps close to a fence running parallel to the burn. The latter route is simpler to follow in mist and interferes less with local farming activities.

After crossing Hareshaw House's tarmac approach road at GR 842871, the route heads northwards to meet the old route. A grassy track then continues to the B6320 Bellingham to Otterburn road next to an old colliery, which closed in the 1950s.

LOUGH SHAW

A track climbs the heather-cloaked slopes to the summit of Lough Shaw. The ridges hereabouts can be marshy in places but nothing like those of the Dark Peak, so far behind us now, or the Cheviots still to come. If the weather is fine, the mood will be an optimistic one, for these are the loftiest hills for miles and thus can offer wide-sweeping panoramas. In the skyline beyond the Redesdale Valley and its low afforested craggy knolls is the main Cheviot range - still a long way off but close enough to whet the appetite.

Beyond Lough Shaw the tracks veer to the left, visiting the top of Deer Play. Ahead lie the heathery hills of Lord's Shaw and Padon Hill. The latter is easily recognized by the beehive monument crowning its summit. The route shown on the OS maps as going north-westwards then north to Lord's Saw does not exist underfoot and it is better to follow the well-defined course traversing marshy ground at the head of Tofts

On Lough Shaw.

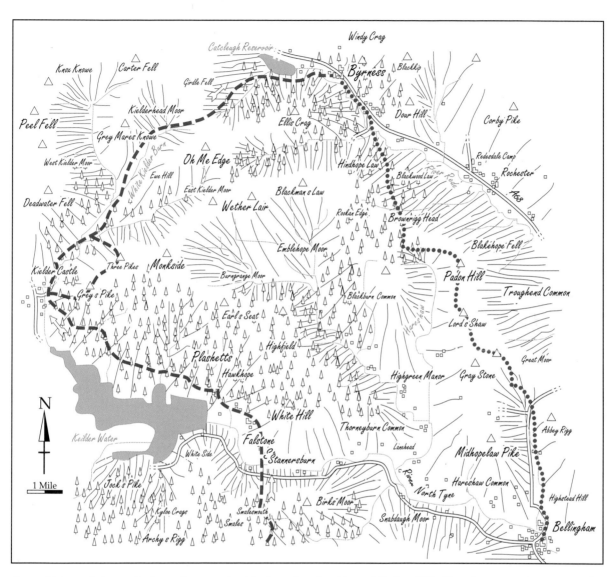

Burn (this path is marked on the map by black and white dotted lines). Be careful not to take the shooters track, which actually descends into the valley of Tofts Burn.

PADON HILL

From Lord's Shaw you can either follow the ridge fence or continue north-westwards on a bold track through the heather. Both meet at a minor road by a cattle grid. From here the path maintains direction on the west side of a fence and climbs gradually on the shoulder of Padon Hill. For those wanting to see the huge cairn erected in 1920 by the Morrison-Bells of Otterburn Hall, a stile in the barbed-wire fence allows access over the heathery summit.

Most will continue in earnest, descending to the saddle beneath Brownrigg Head before climbing on what can be a muddy little path at the edge of the privately owned Gibshiel plantation. The old route used to descend from Padon Hill to Gibshiel Farm and then take the flinted forestry road all the way to Byrness. In my opinion it is drier and faster than the official line,

The gigantic beehive cairn on Padon Hill.

which prolongs the route for just one more moorland lump.

REDESDALE FOREST

The official route follows the fence from Brownrigg Head north-westwards at the edge of the huge conifer plantations before entering them on a wide grassy ride. The Forestry Enterprise's own plantation is met at Rookengate (GR 799955). Here a wide flinted forestry track continues northwards through the conifer corridors of the Redesdale Forest. The route is straight for-

The church at Byrness.

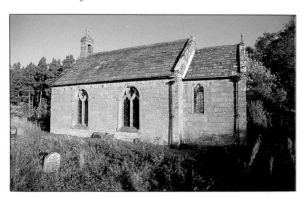

ward - always straight ahead. Byrness now seems close at hand as a fast and easy pace can be maintained. Glimpses of the crag-fringed Byrness Hill and Ravens Knowe are visible through gaps in the spruce woods and soon we are crossing the River Rede at Blakehopeburnhough Farm. At one time this was in the *Guinness Book of Records* as being the longest name in England but more recent maps suggest that the neighbouring farm, Cottonshopeburnfoot is one name and not two, thus beating it by a single letter. (Whatsinanameanyway?)

BYRNESS

Immediately after the bridge the route turns left, following a riverside track through delightful mixed woodland before emerging on the open fields of Cottonshopeburnfoot. A concrete bridge spans the River Rede at its confluence with Cottonshope Burn. Turn right before it if you want to take advantage of the farm's bed and breakfast accommodation or the adjacent camp-site, which has a bunkhouse and drying room and also offers bed and breakfast.

The continuing path to Byrness crosses the bridge and re-enters the Redesdale Forest before turning downhill, crossing the Rede once more and passing through the picnic area by the little church of Holy

A BRIEF HISTORY OF KIELDER AND THE NORTH TYNE VALLEY

Kielder Reservoir was built by damming the North Tyne close to its source. Its controversial construction brought fame to an area which, for most of history, had been a backwater of Northumberland. Now the area has been developed a tourist haven. Water sports, hillwalking, orienteering, and other activities are actively encouraged by the authorities.

Life was lived on a much more austere level in previous centuries. In the time of the first settlers, some 8,000 years ago, the area would have been covered by mixed woodland (oak, birch, hazel, pine and alder) to the 2000ft level. The early settlers were hunters and fishermen but the first farming peoples were those of the Neolithic (Stone Age). They would have made small clearings in the dense forests to cultivate crops. Many of their primitive tools such as stone axes and arrows have been excavated and their huge tombs are found on the hillsides.

Waves of invaders, the Anglo-Saxons, Nords and Danes briefly settled here but their clearings were largely abandoned and the land returned to forest. The lands were conquered for Scotland by King David in 1136 and he made his son William the Duke of Northumberland. The Bellingham family were employed as his chief foresters.

More turbulent times followed as the Normans tried to gain control. Although under Henry I they advanced as far as Bellingham and Wark, constructing a line of motte-and-bailey castles, territory in the Falstone and Kielder areas was largely under Scottish control. Several times in the early fourteenth century Robert the Bruce raided and ransacked the lands, killing many locals in the process. Shielings (smallholdings) were abandoned and laid to waste.

For centuries the people of North Tyne were feared for their lawlessness. Feuds and warring over property were common and tales of the border reivers' cunning at stealing horses and cattle from lowland farmers were widespread. The lawlessness was almost certainly responsible for the building of 'bastles' in the area. These fortified farmhouses contained room for livestock on the ground floor with the owner and his family housed on the first floor.

Probably the greatest influence on the North Tyne's people was that of the Greenwich Hospital Governors who, in 1715, were given the lands confiscated from Earl of Derwentwater for his part in the Jacobite Rebellion. As mentioned in the Cross Fell Lead Mines section they were very keen to foster religion, education and improved living standards, and were responsible for the building of chapels, schools, roads and bridges.

The first commercial coal mine was that opened by the Swinburnes of the Lewisburn Valley but the mine opened in 1851 at Plashetts was the first large-scale enterprise in the region. By 1862 a railway had been built from Hexham (on the Newcastle to Carlisle line) to Hawick and the Scottish Borders, passing through the North Tyne Valley. It was used to transport the coal. The community of Plashetts grew to around 200 people. Unfortunately, after the strike of 1926 the shafts became flooded and were never fully reopened. In 1930 the owner Joseph Slater visited the mines to see what progress had been made on draining the levels. He was tragically killed, overcome by gas, and the mine was finally closed. The railway was closed in 1956. All that remains of the village are a few foundations hidden by thick grass and the sprucewoods of the Kielder Forests.

Although the estates of the North Tyne were planting forests of spruce, fir and birch towards the end of the nineteenth century, the main plantations of the Forestry Commission began in the 1930s following the purchase of lands from the Duke of Northumberland. Today the forest canopy covers 50,000 hectares – the largest man-made forest in Northern Europe. Sitka spruce, the dominant tree, is supplemented by Norway spruce, Larch, Scots pine and Lodgepole pine. Various broad-leaved trees are now also being planted.

The decision to build a reservoir at Kielder stemmed from Tyneside's industrial expansion in the 1960s. Construction began in 1975 and it was opened seven years later. The 1,250 yd long dam holds back 44,000 gallons of water.

PLASHETTS

Trinity. The Byrness Hotel, which offers bar meals and accommodation, lies across the A68 Newcastle-Jedbergh road. The main village, a forestry settlement, lies half a mile north-west, just off the busy highway. Here the youth hostel has been modified from one of the Forestry Enterprise houses.

KIELDER WATER TO BYRNESS
The Alternative route

The alternative route begins with yet more forest, although now highlighted by periodic sightings of Kielder's lake. The prospects improve on the crossing of Kielder Head Moor for this is superb wild country - a return to the mountains.

STANNERSBURN
From Stannersburn village, the reservoir road is followed to the huge Kielder Dam, which is then crossed to the north side. Here a wide, waymarked Forestry Road is used to circumvent the northern shores of the reservoir. At one time there were busy coal mining communities at Plashetts and Hawkhope but the relics

of this industry are largely obscured by the new world of forest and lake. If you are lucky you might spot a pine marten or goshawk, but the desire will be to press on and head for the hills.

KIELDER
From Gowanburn, the road is metalled and descends steadily to Kielder village. The Bathekin Dam seen below was constructed to keep the shallow western extremities of the reservoir full, for unsightly mudbanks would otherwise surface outside the winter months.

Kielder is dominated by its castle, built in 1771 as a hunting lodge by the Duke of Northumberland but now owned by the Forestry Enterprise and used as an information centre. There are no traces of the original castle in which Lord Percy and his wife Lady Elizabeth are said to have taken refuge when fleeing from the troops of Queen Elizabeth I during the Catholic uprisings of 1569.

KIELDER BURN
The Forestry Enterprise have devised a good courtesy route from Kielder over Castle Hill, Mount Common, Greys Pike and Three Pikes, descending through the forest north-westwards to Kielder (using a footbridge

Descending from Kielder Head into the Chattlehope Valley with Catcleugh Reservoir in the distance.

over Ridge End Burn). Although it is a fine route with lovely views of both reservoir and moor, it does involve a great deal of ascent that is subsequently lost.

It is probably more prudent to follow the toll road on the western side of Kielder Burn or forestry tracks on the east side. A right of way then circumvents East Kielder Farm, from where a trackless course traverses fields in the wide valley of the Kielder Burn. The lively river meanders at the edge of the huge spruce plantations clothing the lower slopes of Deadwater Fell, a peak bedecked with a profusion of communications masts.

KIELDER HEAD MOOR

The river divides at Kielder Head and our route follows the White Kielder Burn. This is forded by Kielder Head Farm, an old dwelling now serving as a mountain bothie. The scenery becomes wilder as the path delves deeper into the quiet hills. Soon we are following narrow paths through heather. The valley has closed in, crags fringe the hillsides and the occasional gnarled and twisted tree lines the boisterous burn - this is Kielder Head Moor and it is one of the great secrets of Northumberland.

The start of the path that climbs out of the valley is not clear and is confused further by the well-defined shooters' track which climbs boldly to White Crags. The stream is crossed at GR 688009 and a faint path followed eastwards across rough grass and heather to the start of the shooters' track. A hundred yards to the east (trackless initially), high above the stream, a narrow path though the heather is joined and this climbs to Girdle Fell, passing some lovely cataracts and waterfalls *en route*. The quietude of the moors may be disturbed by the cackle of the red or black grouse. The merlin, goshawk and kestrel often patrol the skies hereabouts and it is quite common to see feral goats roaming the high tops.

The terrain across the top of Girdle Fell is also trackless. A few short stakes do exist but it is better to take a bearing (60° east-north-east) to reach the gate in the ridge fence, lying close to a huge sandstone boulder. East of the fence, the track is more distinct and you are walking on the skyline. Nothing separates you from the wide views encompassing the whole Cheviot range and the lower moors of Otterburn. Below are the plantations which have enveloped Chattlehope Burn. Those on its northern banks are Forestry Enterprise and the ones on the opposite banks are private.

Beneath them in the Redesdale Valley is the Catcleugh Reservoir, built at the turn of the century to supply Newcastle's ever-growing needs. At the eastern edge of Girdle Fell, the route descends along a rough grassy forest ride through recent plantations.

CHATTLEHOPE BURN AND THE CATCLEUGH RESERVOIR

At the foot of the spur, beyond a circular stone-built sheep pen and near a pine copse, the route fords Chattlehope Burn. It then skirts the older Forestry Commission plantations before veering eastwards (trackless) over pastureland, passing Chattlehope Farm. Here a track leads by the shores of Catcleugh Reservoir to its dam. This is crossed to reach the busy A68 trunk road, which is followed for a mile into Byrness, where the official route is met.

NB It is possible to vary the route from Kielder to Byrness by climbing on a wide track northwards to Deadwater Fell where an arduous ridge walk continues to Peel Fell and Carter Fell. It is not a right of way and crosses a Site of Special Scientific Interest run by the Nature Conservancy Council who ask that you avoid the area during the breeding season between March and July.

ROUTE FILE			
Maps	OS Landranger (1:50000) No. 80 'Cheviot Hills'.		
Distance and time Official Way			
Official Way	14 miles (23km)		7 hours
Alternative via Kielder	21 miles (33km)		11 hours
Terrain	Mixture of farmland, forest tracks and moor on official route. Lakeside forestry tracks followed by paths over remote heather moors on the alternative routes.		
Accommodation	B&Bs, inn and camp-site at Byrness. Additionally, bothie at Kielder Head on the alternative route.		
Shops	Byrness. Falstone and Kielder on alternative route.		
Tourist Information	The Manor Office, Hallgate, Hexham, Northumberland. NE46 1XD. Tel. 00434 605225 or for Kielder alternative route -Tower Knowe, Kielder Water, Northumberland NE48 1BY. TEL 0434 240398.		

15

THE LONG RIDGE
Byrness to Kirk Yetholm

This 27 mile (43km) section is the most arduous since scaling Cross Fell and some believe of the whole Pennine Way. Backpackers strike camp at their convenience but other accommodation is well off route and means quitting the ridge.

It makes a pleasant change to stride on open fell-sides after fiddling about over farmland and forest. The complex series of ridges, spurs and side valleys make the Cheviots a fascinating range but this complexity makes viable alternative routes impossible, except those which abandon the ridge.

The Cheviots' remoteness is seldom in doubt, especially in the middle regions. Windy Gyle heralds the change from hill to mountain. It has all the trimmings - a distinctive profile with huge, stony summit cairn, a shelter and superb views. Beyond Windy Gyle the walk becomes tougher and the terrain can be marshy. A diversion to the Cheviot itself can, outside hot summer months, be a real grind. Unless you are masochist it is not worth the effort. It is better to make for Auchope Cairn and The Schil, two fine craggy tops with firm terrain.

The northern outliers become gentle and more verdant, allowing a little comfort for those limbs on the last triumphant march into the quiet Scottish border village of Kirk Yetholm.

Opposite: The Harthope Valley from the eastern slopes of The Cheviot.   *Below: Looking back to Auchope Cairn from the Schil.*

BYRNESS TO KIRK YETHOLM
The Official Route

BYRNESS HILL

The day starts as it means to go on - with a stiff challenge. The way to the ridge and Byrness Hill is unrelentingly steep. A tarmac drive leading from the road fifty yards north-west of the Byrness Hotel is followed until a gate by Byrness Cottage leads to the forest. The grassy rides, bound by rows of mixed conifers bracken and crag, are followed on a bold course up the steep slopes.

At the exit from the forest we are confronted by crags and outcrops, which fringe the hill's summit. A short scramble and the ridge is gained. Here one of many red Ministry of Defence notices warns against straying from the route when red flags are displayed. Beyond the notice is the wide side valley of Cottonshope which, like much of the land in this vicinity, belongs to the Ministry. From the ridge there are superb retrospective views over Redesdale including

Green Crag, Houx Hill.   (Photo: Nicola Gillham)

the Catcleugh Reservoir, surrounded by a patchwork of conifer plantations, verdant pastures and rough heather moor. Further south previous routes over Padon Hill and Lord's Shaw can be retraced.

There is a long way to go at this stage and most will dwell only briefly before striding forth over the pale grasslands to Houx Hill where a fence leads the way to

Looking back west along the ridge between Saughy Crag and Byrness Hill above Redesdale.

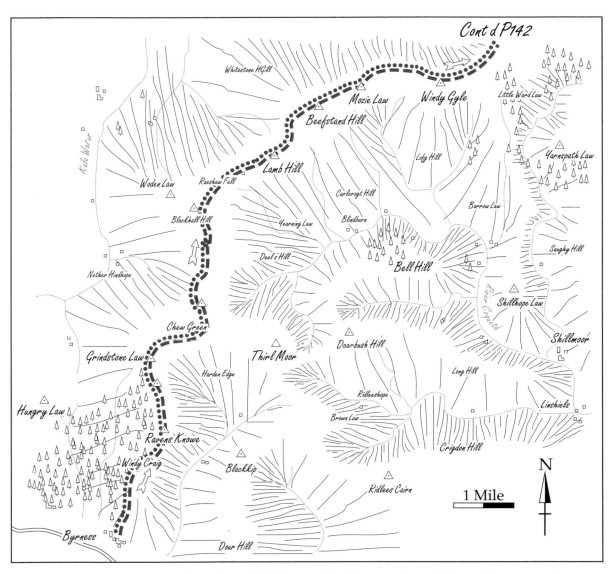

Cont d P142

Ravens Knowe and subsequently to Ogre Hill. The Cheviot massif can be seen on the horizon but is still too distant to be fully appreciated. A descent is made from Ravens Knowe to the border fence between England and Scotland. This lies at the northern extremity of the Redesdale Forest.

CHEW GREEN

After crossing a stile over the border fence we step into Scotland for the first time. The route continues northwards, climbing by a subsidiary fence before turning right (signposted) and descending eastwards across grasslands to Chew Green. This massive complex of ditches and mounds is the remains of a busy Roman camp on Dere Street, an ancient Roman road linking York with the highlands. The present day British Army activities are also evident in the area for they have constructed a metalled road along the line of Gamel's Path to the foot of the ancient fort.

The Pennine Way traces the south and east edges of Chew Green before diverting north eastwards on a faint waymarked track (blue bridleway arrows), which

Striding out on Beefstand Hill with the Schil and The Cheviot dominant on the horizon.

is in fact Dere Street. The ancient road soon becomes more distinct as it veers northwards, skirting Brownhart Law and Black Halls, crossing the border fence twice *en route*. The view into Scotland is riveting. The complex hillscapes surrounding Kale Water and Hindhope Burn are greener than their English counterparts and the hills shapelier. Beyond them the rich plains of the Tweed and Teviotdale lead the eye to the very noticeable twin humps of the Eildon Hills.

Dere Street is abandoned to the north of Black Halls for a narrow track arcing eastwards through grasslands interspersed with heather. Some of the wetter sections have recently been spanned by board-walks - a dubious addition to this lonely wilderness.

LAMB HILL
To the east of Raeshaw Fell the border fence and watershed are rejoined and the path continues to the Mountain Refuge Hut - a very useful shelter for travellers caught in harsh weather conditions. The way then climbs to Lamb Hill, whose flat summit is furnished with a concrete trig. point. In views ahead the heathery expanse of Beefstand Hill partially obscures the Cheviot but to its left another shapely eminence, Windy Gyle, becomes prominent in the mid-distance.

BEEFSTAND HILL
From Lamb Hill the path closely follows the border fence along the meandering ridge over the summits of

Beefstand Hill and Mozie Law. The Cheviot now begins to dominate surrounding hills, although forming only part of a wide panorama including the Schil and Hedgehope Hill. The Street, another Roman highway, joins the ridge to the east of Mozie Law. It straddles the ridge from the Coquet Valley to the south and Kale Water in the north and can be used as an escape road in either direction. There is a telephone at Windyhaugh (GR 867107) in the Coquet Valley.

WINDY GYLE
The way continues past the head of the splendid Rowhope Valley, where interlocking spurs crowd the meandering burn in a mottled sea of emerald and sage, frequently softened and veiled by the afternoon sun. After a short climb, the summit of Windy Gyle is attained. It is decorated by a huge bouldery cairn, crowned by a concrete trig. point and wind shelter. The cairn is known as Russell's Cairn and is said to commemorate Lord Francis Russell, who was killed here in 1585. Many historians argue that it is a Bronze Age burial mound. The summit is a superb place to be on a clear day. It has good views in all directions - the Cheviot looms large beyond the heathland of Kings Seat and Cairn Hill and the deep nick of Rowhope Burn plots a meandering course through velvet-draped grassy knolls.

A short distance east on the descent from Windy Gyle is another cairn, said by some to be the true

(Photo: Nicola Gillham)

Above: Russell's Cairn on the summit of Windy Gyle.

Below: Hen Hole beneath Auchope Cairn.

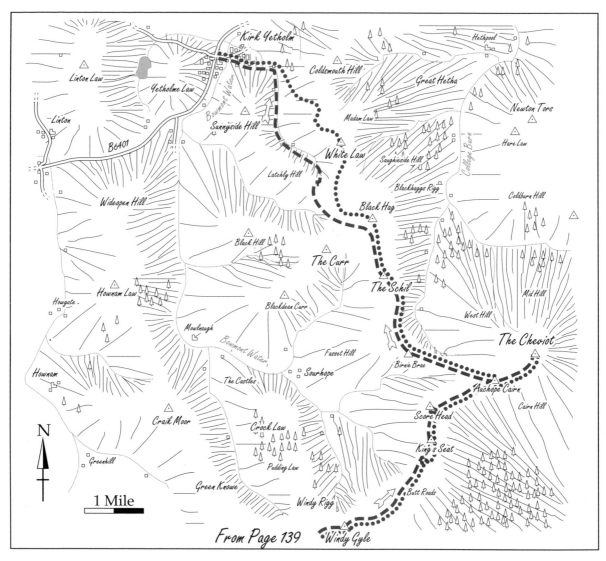

From Page 139

Russell's Cairn. From here the conifer plantations of Uswayford (pronounced Oosyford) have concealed the barren hillslopes and detracted from the wilderness atmosphere.

A drovers' route known as Clennell Street can be used by those who wish to vacate the ridge and look for accommodation. It straddles the ridge at a cairn (GR 872160) and leads southwards direct to Uswayford Farm where, at the time of writing, bed and breakfast is offered - book well in advance to be sure of a place. In the opposite direction the old road descends from a ladder stile in the border fence to Cocklawfoot where a narrow, lightly used lane leads through the beautiful Bowmont Valley to Kirk Yetholm. (10 miles from the ridge).

CAIRN HILL

For those hardy souls who aim to carry on, the path continues over rough, heather-clad peatlands to Kings Seat, where the long, arduous ascent to Cairn Hill begins. The ground can be horribly boggy after periods of rain but the going is made easier by the gradual addition of board walks. To many these are alien, although at this stage in the proceedings, few weary

Summit rocks, The Schil.

Pennine Wayers will summon up enough resolve to grumble.

At a fence corner (GR 897195) is the start of an officially recommended detour to the Cheviot. It will add three miles (4.8km) to an already lengthy day and, although macho men and masochists will find the challenge irresistible, few others will bother. Although some of the worst sections are now paved with stone slabs, The Cheviot's top is still a peat-hagged morass with little to recommend its inclusion from this direction. Much better to leave it for a day-walk from the College Valley or Langleeford.

AUCHOPE CAIRN

The more direct route continues on duck-boards from Cairn Hill northwards to Auchope Cairn. This pleasing top, furnished with a couple of stone cairns and a good shelter, is firmly in the shadow of the sprawling dark mass of the Cheviot. In the opposite direction, however, there are splendid views. Centre-stage, and rising from the lonely upper regions of the College Valley, is the Schil, a rock-crested, domed peak forming the highest part of a ridge to be used on the final descent to Kirk Yetholm.

HEN HOLE

From Auchope Cairn the route descends westwards on a spur between the Cheviot and College Burns. The latter tumbles down from the big Cheviot into a rocky declivity known as Hen Hole. A short detour can be made to the rocks overlooking the spectacular chasm, which has been designated a nature reserve because of an abundance of rare flowers, ferns and mosses. This mystical place is the subject of many a tale and is said to have been the home of fairies who were lured to their death by curious music. Another inhabitant was Black Adam, who was said to have invaded a wedding party at Wooperton, robbed the guests and stabbed the bride before retreating. He was pursued by the irate bridegroom and both were killed attempting to jump the gorge.

The path continues, without jumping any gorges, to the recently constructed Mountain Refuge Hut, which can offer shelter to those who are too tired to continue.

THE SCHIL

After rounding the head of College Burn and passing above a plantation of spruce, the Schil stands proud in the view ahead, barring the way to journeys end. It is a fine hill, one of the Cheviots' best, but most Pennine Way travellers will wish it was somewhere else. Most supreme efforts are rewarded, however, and from the 30ft mound of crag and boulder that tops the summit we can spy over the rounded Cheviot outliers to the wide plains of the Scottish Lowlands and Northumbrian coast.

BLACK HAG

An easy-paced descent down grassy slopes leads to Black Hag, where a signpost marks the divergence of

Approaching the Iron-Age fort on Green Humbleton above Kirk Yetholm.

the high and low-level alternative routes. The high level route has been recently devised and, although scenically superior, it is harder, having quite a few undulations in its ridges. Many weary souls opt for the old (low-level) route described later.

The right fork is taken for the high route and this

straddles Black Hag's western shoulder to rejoin the border fence before descending the spur of Steer Rigg.

WHITE LAW

The climb to White Law is quite steep and just as unwelcome as that on the Schil but now we are at least on the last lap! Splendid views include the Halterburn Valley and the chequered field patterns of the Tweed Valley. Kirk Yetholm is unfortunately out of view - hidden by the slopes of Staerough Hill. To the east beyond the distinctive tops of the Northern Cheviot foothills the Northumbrian coastline is clearly visible.

The border fence continues to guide progress to GR 854268. Here a signposted grassy cart track leads north-westwards to join the Halterburn Valley road beneath Green Humbleton, whose top is scored by the earthworks of an Iron Age fort.

KIRK YETHOLM

The road will be followed to Kirk Yetholm and journey's end but there is one last hurdle: it climbs 150 ft before that last decline to the Border Hotel.

The village green at Kirk Yetholm.

The Halterburn Valley - once the main route of the Pennine Way. It is now listed as a foul weather alternative.

BLACK HAG TO KIRK YETHOLM
Official Foul Weather Alternative

BLACK HAG

An old green road to the left of the main ridge route curves gently round the head of the valley of the Rowhope Burn. Views back to the Schil are attractive and one can take a last look at the big Cheviot before descending to the col between Black Hag and Latchly Hill.

HALTERBURN VALLEY

The wide track continues down to Curr Burn but it is left for a route which goes through the gate at the col and then descends on the bracken-clad slopes at the head of the Halterburn Valley. The valley bottom is reached at Old Halterburn Head Farm, which lies in ruins, surrounded by trees and tightly enclosed by grassy hillsides.

A farm road then leads to Burnhead, the first habitation passed since leaving Byrness. The farmyard is kept to the right. Kirk Yetholm is now only 3 miles (4.8km) distant and, although out of view, obscured still by Staerough Hill, its presence is felt. Further north, the combination of excitement at successfully completing this Pennine Way challenge, the lure of that promised half pint 'on Wainwright', and an easy tar-

mac lane seem to give the extra energy necessary for faster motion. It is easy to ignore the pain but also the scenery. The narrow banks of the Halterburn are, in places, covered with the yellow and scarlet blooms of the musk, a flower which mystified the scientists by losing its scent soon after being introduced to this country.

The high-level route is met beneath the steep flanks of Green Humbleton and we are left with that last steep hurdle before striding into Kirk Yetholm.

ROUTE FILE

Maps	OS Landranger (1:50000) Nos 80. 'Cheviot Hills' and 74 'Kelso'
Distance and time Official Way including the Cheviot	25 miles (40km) 15 hours 27 miles (44km) 16 hours
Terrain	High mountain ridges. Boggy in the region of the Cheviot although stone flags now straddle the worst of the bogs.
Accommodation	B&Bs at Uswayford Farm. Youth hostel, inns, B&Bs and camp-site at Yetholm.
Shops	Post Office at Byrness will be the last available until Town Yetholm at journey's end.
Tourist Information	Murray's Green, Jedburgh, Roxburghshire, TD18 6BE. Tel. 0835 63435.

Appendix 1

ROUTE VARIATIONS
1 - THE EAST DALES LOOP

In the main text I have tried to make the various routes converge at convenient 'valley' centres. Unfortunately much of the land between Hawes and Tan Hill is 'out of bounds' and, with few rights of way available I was stuck for a logical alternative.

Further east the situation improves. The moors are still dedicated to the great grouse hunters but they are traversed with a network of old roads, bridleways and footpaths. I therefore decided to offer an East Dales Loop route, which, although well away from the main Pennine watershed, still retained the mountain-walking theme of the 'Way'. It is a splendid route in its own right and probably scenically superior to the other itineraries.

Opposite: Flinter Gill Falls near Dent (see Howgill route on page 156).

Below: Climbing out of Swaledale above Barney Beck.

KETTLEWELL TO AYSGARTH

Distance 14 miles (22km)
This superb day begins with the exploration of Buckden Pike, one of Yorkshire's highest peaks, and continues in fine fashion, visiting the peaceful pastures of the Walden Valley and the waterfalls of Aysgarth.

The alternative route from Kettlewell to Buckden Pike is described in Chapter 7.

BUCKDEN PIKE
After traversing eastwards from the summit (trackless), the Walden Road is joined once more and this descends north-eastwards into the remote fellsides at the head of the Walden Valley. Deepdale Gill is forded, close to the confluence with Fosse Gill and the route continues along the western banks of the combined waters, which are now known as Walden Beck.

THE WALDEN VALLEY
The waymarked bridleway meets the terminus of a metalled road at Kentucky House (farm). At GR

Looking into the Walden Valley.

002819 a footpath signposted 'to Cote Bridge' points the way across fields towards West Burton. The path continues parallel to the river, crossing walls too numerous to mention via gates and gap stiles to reach the road near Cote Farm (GR 017857).

After turning right along the road, Cote Bridge is crossed and a cart track on its far side leads by the banks of Walden Beck to meadowland. The beck is recrossed at another footbridge and the succeeding

West Burton, the first village encountered on the East Dales Loop from Buckden Pike.

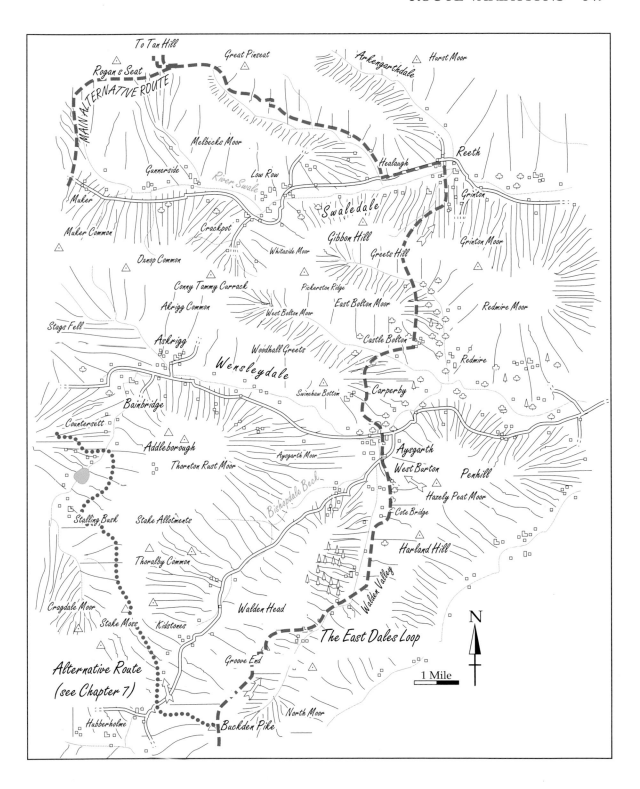

The Middle Falls Aysgarth.

path reaches the road a short way to the south of West Burton.

WEST BURTON

West Burton is a peaceful and lovely village. An expansive triangular green separates rows of stone cottages. On the green is an obelisk, which, surprisingly, commemorates nought. The excellent Fox and Hounds Inn would be a good choice for those seeking accommodation.

Before leaving it would be a worthwhile detour to see the waterfalls which lie to the east of the village. Here in a sylvan hollow the waters of Walden Beck thrust through a nick in dark mossy rocks to form a superb cascade.

For those who want to continue to Aysgarth, a ginnel at the far side of the green and signposted 'to the road for Eshington Bridge' leads to the B-road. Immediately opposite, beyond a gate, a footpath crosses fields, passing to the left of a stone barn. It briefly acquaints itself with the banks of Bishopdale Beck before veering right to the road near Eshington Bridge (GR 015878). Beyond the bridge a stile on the left

hand side of the road marks the start of a path, which climbs north-north-westerly across meadows to the A684 at Aysgarth.

AYSGARTH

Unlike West Burton, Aysgarth village has been commercialized, but is nevertheless an attractive place. The beauty is evident on descending a tree-lined drive past the fine nineteenth-century church to the valley bottom at Yore Bridge. From here you can see the boisterous River Ure crashing over wide rocky ledges in an impressive series of cataracts, known collectively as the Upper Falls.

AYSGARTH TO REETH

Distance 10 miles (17km)

Leaving Aysgarth across the Yore Bridge, a path commences along the west side of the National Trust car park. After climbing some steps to a kissing gate it straddles the embankment of a disused railway and

Descending into Reeth from Greets Hill.

thence across fields to meet the Carperby road, just short of the village. The television vet, James Herriot, and his wife Helen spent their honeymoon at the Wheatsheaf Inn, which lies beyond the green.

Our route turns left at the near side of the green, following a walled lane, marked 'to other footpaths'. Beyond a gate a left turn leads into a field. A stile in the far wall gives access to a rutted vehicle track which leads to the foot of some crags. Here we head east-north-east on a bridleway before turning left on meeting a walled lane climbing from the village. A right fork signposted 'to Castle Bolton' then climbs to lofty pastures with fine views down the length of Wensleydale.

Two streams are forded, the first of which can be awkward when in spate. The second crossing is of a feeder stream, which tumbles into the narrow wooded glen of Beldon Beck.

CASTLE BOLTON AND GREETS HILL
The track then veers left to a gate near a wall corner, where it makes a beeline for Castle Bolton, whose large square keep can be spotted through some tall trees. The castle, built in 1379 by the first Lord Scrope,

Chancellor of England, has had a turbulent history. In 1568 Mary Queen of Scots was imprisoned within its walls. In 1645 Royalists were besieged by Parliamentary forces who, two years later, had it partially dismantled. In 1761 the north-east tower, which had been severely weakened in the process, collapsed after a great storm.

Our route passes between the castle and the church to reach the long village green. On the north side of the green, near a telephone box and opposite a cottage named Valley View (B&B), a winding walled lane climbs to high pastures where it resumes as a rutted track offering the last views of Wensleydale, which are dominated by Penhill.

The brow of the hill is attained and we overlook the depression of Apedale. Gone are the lush pastures of Wensleydale, replaced by expansive heather moors, rent by a narrow swathe of grassland at the valley bottom.

The track, now stony, descends to cross the bridge over Apedale Beck, passing a remote shooting hut and sheep-pens before climbing to Greets Hill. The summit, littered with spoil heaps from defunct lead-mining

Approaching the lead mines near Surrender Bridge north-west of Reeth.

activities, is a fine viewpoint for the Northern Dales and County Durham's coastal plains.

A cairned grassy track, indistinct in places, descends north-eastwards over stony slopes to meet a moorland lane at GR 038964. The village of Reeth can be seen nestling on a verdant shelf at the meeting of Swaledale and Arkengarthdale and beneath the pale, crag-fringed flanks of Fremington Edge and the shapely Calver Hill, which dominate the skyline.

GRINTON AND REETH
The lane is followed for a couple of hundred yards

ing through an area of bracken to a ladder stile at the roadside above Grinton (GR 046978).After descending the lane for a couple of hundred yards, the pleasant village of Grinton is reached and we pass its inn and square-towered parish church. The River Swale is crossed on an impressive three-arched bridge.

A footpath on the left hand side of the road beyond the bridge now takes us across fields, passing to the left of a farmhouse before tracing the banks of Arkle Beck to the road just short of Reeth's centre.

Reeth is a lively place. A few large hotels and rows of stone-built cottages are built round a huge triangular green. Much of the village's initial prosperity grew from the fruits of lead mining and, at one time, its population grew to over 1,300. It is down to 350 now and tourism has taken over as the main industry. The inhabitants are geared to making you very welcome indeed. There is a bank, a good shop and a café. This is certainly a good place to spend the night.

REETH TO BOWES OR TAN HILL

Distance 18 miles (29km) to Bowes
12 miles (20km) to Tan Hill

The most direct route northwards would certainly be to use valley paths down Arkengarthdale and across West Moor to Sleightholme and Bowes. This is a very scenic route and would be a good option in bad weather. Somehow though, it would betray the Pennine Way theme and so my chosen path heads for the hills to meet the alternative route at Sleightholme or Tan Hill.

From the green in Reeth (by Barclay's Bank), follow the sign 'to the river' to Quaker Lane where a path 'to Healaugh' is followed across meadowland to join the banks of the Swale. After about a mile the lovely riverside path is abandoned for one to the village of Healaugh. A walled path by the telephone box then leads to more meadows, which are traversed westwards to meet a lane lined with tall broad-leaved trees.

BARNEY BECK and SURRENDER BRIDGE
Beyond Thiernswood Hall the lane becomes a track and continues through some woodland. At a sharp bend it is left for a path beyond a gap stile in the wall to the left. It continues north-westwards across verdant pastures close to the wall above the tree-filled ravine of Barney Beck. A small gate in the wall then allows entry

until a left turn is made along a wide track for a few yards. A grassy path then descends north-north-east past some grouse butts and through heathland. After passing a white post and crossing a wide cart track, a faint path leads towards the cutting of Grinton Gill. It follows the edge past a large sheepfold before descend-

into the woodland and the narrow path traces the upper edge with glimpses of the lively stream far below.

The deep cutting of a feeder stream, Bleaberry Gill (GR 996999) is encountered and the path descends to ford the stream before climbing to the edge of rough moorland. The woods of Barney Gill have now ceased and the shallow stream flows in the bare stony environs of the Surrender lead mines. The path descends into the ravine past the old smelting mill to reach a high moorland road at the one-arched Surrender Bridge.

OLD GANG MINES

We briefly share our route with Wainwright's Coast to Coast route. It heads along the gravel road on the northern banks of Old Gang Beck. You are never very far away from the relics of lead-mining but the rural charm of birdsong and wildflowers is also in abundance. A fast pace is obtained on the well-graded track and soon the Old Gang smelt mill is reached. Several buildings, including a blacksmith's shop and a furnace lie crumbled by the lively beck. The crumbling has probably now been arrested by some timely restoration work.

HARD LEVEL GILL

Beyond the smelt mill the stream becomes Hard Level Gill. At the second junction of tracks near the ruin of Level House, we turn left, crossing via the one-arched Level House Bridge. Here we climb out of the valley parallel to North Rake Hush (not named on 1:50000 maps). The alternative route northwards to Bowes (or Tan Hill) via Punchard Moor (trackless hereabouts) is met by a large cairn as a track from Moor House joins from the left. (*See* Chapter 8 Alternative Route.)

ROUTE FILE

Maps	OS Landranger (1:50000) Nos 98 and 92 or Outdoor Leisure Map (1:25000) No. 30 'Yorkshire Dales North & Central'
Distance and time	
To Bowes	42 miles (68km) 24 hours (3 days)
To Tan Hill	36 miles (59km) 22 hours (3 days)
Accommodation	Youth Hostel at Aysgarth, Grinton. Inns and B&Bs at West Burton, Aysgarth, Carperby, Castle Bolton, Grinton, Reeth, Healaugh and Bowes. An inn at Tan Hill. Camp-sites at West Burton, Aysgarth and Bowes.
Shops	At West Burton, Aysgarth, Carperby, Castle Bolton, Reeth, Healaugh and Bowes.

2 - OTHER ALTERNATIVE ROUTES

There are numerous other routes which deserve consideration but there is just not enough space to describe them in detail. I therefore decided to throw in a few brief itineraries for good measure.

HORTON-IN-RIBBLESDALE TO DUFTON
Via the Howgills, Wild Boar Fell and Kirkby Stephen

Distance 55 miles (89km)
Extra Maps needed No 97 (Kendal & Morecambe)
A diversion could be made from Old Ing Farm north of Horton-in-Ribblesdale (North Yorkshire, Landranger 98 GR SD 804773) north-westwards to Ribblehead, passing the famous viaduct before traversing the Great Wold north of Whernside to the pretty village of Dent. The route would continue on riverside paths before straddling the Frostrow Fells to Sedbergh.

A superb climb would then follow over the much-loved Howgill Fells via Winder, the Calders and Great Dummacks, descending by the spectacular Cautley Crags and Cautley Spout waterfalls. Wild Boar Fell could be climbed via either the Upper Rawthey Valley and Swarth Fell. or Fell End Clouds. Fell End Clouds is one of the pleasantest limestone peaks outside the Yorkshire Dales.

Footpaths through the pastoral Mallerstang would then lead to Kirkby Stephen. Either country lanes or paths through the Eden Valley would then have to be followed to Dufton (Cumbria- Landranger 91, GR NY 688251), where the official Pennine Way is rejoined. The *Alternative Pennine Way* by Denis Brook and Phil Hinchcliffe (Cicerone) offers such a route for those who do not fancy the hassle of picking there own waythrough the maze of low moor, farmland and country lanes.

ADVANTAGES AND DISADVANTAGES
The Howgills and Wild Boar Fell offer some of the finest hill walks in the Pennines but the Ministry of Defence firing ranges of Warcop prevent an early entry on to the North Pennines, thus necessitating a long valley walk north of Kirkby Stephen. To many walkers, this would contradict the theme of the Pennine Way.

MIDDLETON-in-TEESDALE TO NINEBANKS via Burnhope Seat

Distance 28 miles (45km)
No extra maps needed.
This high-level alternative omitting Cross Fell would divert from the official Pennine Way at Holwick Head Bridge (GR NY 889283 Landranger 91). A country lane climbs to Scar End, Ettersgill where a footpath climbs rough moorland slopes to the ridge at Swinhope Head.

A long and arduous ridge walk over Frendrith Hill Chapelfell Top and Coldberry End reaches its highest peak at Burnhope Seat 2448ft (746m). From here there is a gradual descent to the A689 road at the high pass of Killhope Cross and thence over Slate Hill and Black Hill. A bridleway traversing the slopes of The Dodd and Middle Rigg descends to the beautiful West Allen Valley at Ninebanks (GR NY 783533 Landranger 87), where there is a youth hostel. Alternatively the route could descend from Killhope Law to Coalcleugh and enter East Allendale via Hartley Moor.

ADVANTAGES AND DISADVANTAGES
This traverses many miles of grouse moor with few rights of way. The route is miry in place and very arduous, although less circuitous than the Cross Fell itinerary. It is also very dull. In misty conditions navigation would be present some difficulties.

Page 154/5: Cautley Crag.

BYRNESS TO KIRK YETHOLM
via Alwinton

Distance

Byrness to Alwinton	*18 miles (29km)*
Alwinton to Kirk Yetholm	*19 miles (30km)*

No extra maps needed.

The official way is followed to GR NT 791097 (Landranger No. 80) east of Brownhart Law. A right turn (east) along a Landrover track continues to Deels Fell then descends to Blindburn Farm. From here you can continue eastwards along a metalled lane, closely following the River Coquet through a narrow, twisting valley to the village of Alwinton, where you can stop for the night. If time allows a brief but interesting diversion from the road could be used on the marked footpath from Shillmoor Farm (GR 886077) to GR 906065 west of Alwinton.

On the next day the Clennell Street (old Roman road) is used to climb through fell and forest to attain the main Cheviot ridge east of Windy Gyle. It is feasible either to continue along the Pennine Way to Kirk Yetholm or descend via Cocklawfoot into the Beaumont Valley where a narrow country lane leads northwards to Kirk Yetholm.

ADVANTAGES AND DISADVANTAGES

The route explores some very interesting corners of the Cheviots, especially the Upper Coquet Valley. It also splits up that long final leg. It is, however very circuitous and involves some walking on tarmac.

Cocklawfoot near the Bowmont Valley north of the Cheviot Ridge.

APPENDIX 2

PLANNING THE TRIP

The Pennine Way is one of the finest and most challenging of Britain's long-distance routes. It is still a serious expedition and should not be underestimated. The successful Pennine Way walker should be reasonably fit and fully practised in the use of map and compass.

Make sure you are fully equipped with strong boots and a good waterproof jacket and overtrousers. Getting cold and wet on a high-level walk renders you vulnerable to hypothermia. Try to keep the load in your rucksack down to 30lb (13.5kg) if you are camping and less if you're hostelling or using bed and breakfast establishments.

The maps in the book are not intended to be used in the field. Although beautifully drawn they lack the detail required to navigate safely through the mountains. The scales of the maps vary for the convenience of the layout.

Although I have split the book into fifteen chapters it is not a recommended schedule. Experienced long-distance walkers would easily be able to cover these distances but most walkers seem to take about three weeks, including the odd rest day. Choose the itinerary to match your own ability.

USEFUL READING

Pennine Way Companion - A. W. Wainwright (Michael Joseph)
Pennine Way North & South (2 vols) - Tony Hopkins (Aurum Press)
England's Last Wilderness -David Bellamy & Richard Quayle (Michael Joseph)
Mountains & Moorland - W.H. Pearsall (Collins)
Walking the Dales - Mike Harding (Michael Joseph)
The Alternative Pennine Way - Denis Brook & Phil Hinchcliffe (Cicerone)
An Introduction to the History of Upper North Tynedale _ Norman McCord (Northumbrian Water)
Walking in the North Pennines - Paddy Dillon (Cicerone)
The Pennine Mountains - Terry Marsh (Hodder)

PLANNING FILE

STAGE FROM/TO	DISTANCE IN MILES OFFICIAL	ALTERNTIVE
Edale to Crowden	16	17
Crowden to Standedge	11	12
Standedge to the Calder Valley	14	15
The Calder Valley to Lothersdale	18	21
Lothersdale to Malham	15	18
Malham to Horton-in-Ribbplesdale	14	-
Malham to Kettlewell	-	10
Horton-in-Ribblesdale to Hawes	14	-
Kettlewell to Hawes	-	17
Hawes to Tan Hill	16	19
Tan Hill to Middleton-in-Teesdale	16	n/a
Middleton-in-Teesdale to Dufton	17	-
Middleton-in-Teesdale to Alston	-	20
Dufton to Alston	19	-
Alston to Hadrian's Wall	16	21
Hadrian's Wall to Bellingham	21	-
Hadrian's Wall to Kielder	-	17
Bellingham to Byrness	14	-
Kielder to Byrness	-	21
Byrness to Kirk Yetholm	25	n/a

EAST DALES LOOP ALTERNATIVE		
Kettlewell to Aysgarth		14
Aysgarth to Reeth		10
Reeth to Bowes		18

ORDNANCE SURVEY MAPS REQUIRED

1:50000 Landranger Series :-
Nos 110; 109; 103; 104*; 98; 91; 86; 80 and 74. No. 92 would also be required for the Bowes Loop and also the East Dales Loop unless the Outdoor Leisure Map No. 30 was purchased.

Useful Outdoor Leisure Maps (1:25000) which cover some of the route are Nos 1 Dark Peak; 21 South Pennines; 2,10 and 30 Yorkshire Dales; and 31 Teesdale.

* would not be needed if Outdoor Leisure Map No 10. were purchased.

TRANSPORT

Edale is well served by the Manchester to Sheffield railway service. At the end of the Pennine Way, buses run between Kirk Yetholm and Kelso where a further bus service goes to Berwick-upon-Tweed. Berwick is on the main London Kings Cross to Edinburgh railway.

INDEX